MW01453489

AIDS

Look for these and other books in the Lucent Overview Series:

Abortion
Adoption
AIDS
Alcoholism
Artificial Organs
The Brain
Cancer
Censorship
Child Abuse
Children's Rights
Cities
Dealing with Death
Death Penalty
Democracy
Drug Abuse
Eating Disorders
Environmental Groups
Espionage
Ethnic Violence
Euthanasia
Extraterrestrial Life
Family Violence
Gangs

Gay Rights
Genetic Engineering
Gun Control
Hate Groups
Homeless Children
Homelessness
Illegal Immigration
Illiteracy
Immigration
Juvenile Crime
Memory
Mental Illness
Organ Transplants
Police Brutality
Population
Poverty
Prisons
Schools
Smoking
Suicide
Women's Rights
World Hunger

AIDS

by Lori Shein

LUCENT BOOKS

LUCENT *Overview Series*

Lucent Overview Series

Library of Congress Cataloging-in-Publication Data

Shein, Lori, 1957–
    AIDS / by Lori Shein.
       p. cm. — (Lucent overview series)
    Includes bibliographical references and index.
    Summary: An overview of AIDS including information about its discovery, methods of prevention, testing for HIV infection, the global epidemic, and what the future holds.
    ISBN 1-56006-193-6 (lib. bdg. : paper)
    1. AIDS (Disease)—Juvenile literature. [1. AIDS (Disease) 2. Diseases.]   I. Title. II. Series.
RC607.A26S485   1998
616.97'92—dc21   98–9461
                                                                       CIP
                                                                        AC

No part of this book may be reproduced or used in any form or by any means, electrical, mechanical, or otherwise, including, but not limited to, photocopy, recording, or any information storage and retrieval system, without prior written permission from the publisher.

Copyright © 1998 by Lucent Books, Inc.
P.O. Box 289011, San Diego, CA 92198-9011
Printed in the U.S.A.

Contents

INTRODUCTION	6
CHAPTER ONE Unraveling the Mystery	11
CHAPTER TWO The Challenge of Preventing AIDS	24
CHAPTER THREE Testing for HIV Infection	37
CHAPTER FOUR The Global Epidemic	54
CHAPTER FIVE Is the End in Sight?	65
NOTES	83
GLOSSARY	89
ORGANIZATIONS TO CONTACT	92
SUGGESTIONS FOR FURTHER READING	99
WORKS CONSULTED	102
INDEX	107
PICTURE CREDITS	111
ABOUT THE AUTHOR	112

Introduction

TWO DECADES AGO, no one had ever heard of HIV or AIDS. Today HIV and AIDS are household words, known to practically every adult and schoolchild—in this country at least. But familiarity with AIDS has eliminated only some of the mystery and almost none of the controversy that accompanied the disease in its earliest days.

There was a time, not long ago, when no one knew for sure what caused AIDS or how it spread. So little was known about the disease that it didn't even have a name until 1982, when the English-speaking world chose "acquired immune deficiency syndrome" (later "acquired immunodeficiency syndrome"), or AIDS. Since that time, however, researchers have learned a great deal about AIDS. They know what causes it and how it spreads. They even know the genetic makeup of HIV, the virus that causes AIDS. And yet they still wrestle with the mystery of how to turn that knowledge and the data from other research into a vaccine or cure.

A magnet for controversy

As for controversy, AIDS continues to be a magnet for moralizing and politicking on issues ranging from lifestyle and sexual orientation to civil liberties and childbirth. New knowledge and heightened awareness have had little effect in this regard. For example, researchers have tested many methods of prevention but there is little agreement either at home or abroad about which methods to use to slow the spread of HIV and AIDS. Experts in the medical and pub-

Marchers in San Francisco take part in an AIDS fund-raiser. Heightened public awareness of AIDS has not lessened the moral and political controversy that surrounds the disease.

lic health communities cannot even agree on whether parents of newborn infants should be told when tests reveal that their babies are HIV-positive.

Drug research has not escaped controversy either. Advocates for people with AIDS often complain about the ploddingly slow release of new drugs for controlled trials and public use. The first drug thought to have any significant effect on the course of the disease—AZT—did not prove to be an ideal treatment. It has debilitating side effects and did not live up to claims made about its ability to halt the disease. But it was given quick approval for public use. Critics have since accused researchers and drug companies of rushing the drug through the development process and into production for financial gain and temporary prestige.

More recent achievements in drug research seem far more promising, but only for those who have access to them. For a few AIDS patients, death can now be postponed for months and even years. Thus some who had painfully come to terms with the prospect of an early death now contemplate renewed life (if only for a while). But this medical achievement has also led to complaints of unfairness. For the new drugs offer hope to only a small number of the world's people. The vast majority who contract HIV worldwide will not live long enough to accumulate the money to pay for the latest drug treatments. Critics decry the circumstances that have resulted in so much time and money spent on treatments that benefit so few.

The human tragedy

These and other controversies have often overshadowed what is—at its core—a human tragedy. Whatever one thinks of AIDS, first and foremost, it is a deadly disease— one that prematurely steals life from young and old, rich and poor, male and female. In the years since medical reseachers first identified AIDS, an estimated 30 million people worldwide have been infected with HIV and more than 6.4 million people have died. No one has attempted to tally the numbers of grieving friends and relatives who are left behind. As H. R. Shepherd, chairman of the Albert B. Sabin Vaccine Foundation, writes, "AIDS takes an incalculable toll on humanity. Millions of grieving families must watch loved ones with the disease suffer pain that exceeds even the most potent drugs' ability to suppress it, their bodies slowly, inexorably atrophying."[1]

Chris is one of those who know firsthand the pain of seeing a loved one waste away from AIDS. When he and Stephen met in Baltimore, Stephen was at work on his doctorate. The two soon moved to Minnesota, where Stephen found work as a clinical supervisor at a family social service agency and Chris continued his career as a computer software engineer. "Life seemed exceptionally good, until Stephen got seriously ill in early 1993," writes author Gail B. Stewart.[2]

Stephen experienced severe diarrhea and pain in his stomach and abdomen. Within three months he had lost sixty-two pounds. He finally went to the hospital, and it was there that he learned that he was suffering from a condition known as cytomegalovirus disease, an ailment commonly found in people with HIV and AIDS. Later tests confirmed that Stephen had been infected with the AIDS virus. When Stephen came down with a near-fatal case of pneumonia shortly afterward, his condition was upgraded to full-blown AIDS.

For a time, Stephen fought the loss of appetite and weight loss, both part of the wasting syndrome that often accompanies AIDS. And with the help of medications, he

Stephen (right) and Chris recall happier days, before Stephen was diagnosed as HIV-positive.

fought the pain that wracked his body. And then, on July 3, 1995, Stephen's battle with AIDS ended. Chris remained by his side in the final moments.

> "I just held his hand, and told him that everybody would be okay. He was spitting up blood from that [pneumonia-infected] lung, and he seemed so panicky, but I just kept trying to calm him down. I just wiped away the blood from his mouth, and talked to him." And then, in a voice choked with emotion, Chris adds, "I miss him so much."[3]

As often happens with events of worldwide significance, such as the appearance and spread of a deadly new disease, it is easy to forget that behind all the numbers and political rhetoric are individuals—men, women, and children. Their stories serve as a reminder of the human toll of AIDS.

1

Unraveling the Mystery

WHEN THE FIRST cases of AIDS surfaced in the United States and Europe in the late 1970s and early 1980s doctors had no idea what they were dealing with. Nearly all the affected patients were previously healthy young men. The medical literature of the time made no mention of this group as likely candidates for the rare forms of pneumonia, skin cancer, and other conditions showing up in the doctors' offices. What the literature did say, however, was that these conditions—rare as they were—hardly ever killed anyone. And yet, one by one, these patients were dying horrible deaths.

The first cases were especially perplexing because they did not fit the pattern of any known disease. They exhibited no common set of symptoms and had no recognizable source. The only common characteristic seemed to be sexual orientation: nearly all of the first AIDS patients were gay men with active sex lives. This link interested the doctors mainly because it suggested that the disease might be sexually transmitted. Sexually transmitted diseases were nothing new; there were plenty of sexually transmitted diseases, and most of those could easily be treated or at least controlled. Doctors hoped that this new and fatal disease, once they figured it out, would cease to be so threatening.

But the mystery went deeper than most people expected. This disease was not like the others, and by the mid-1980s, when dedicated medical professionals and researchers had

A man ravaged by AIDS lies in a New York hospital bed. The first cases of AIDS baffled doctors because the disease did not have a recognizable source or common set of symptoms.

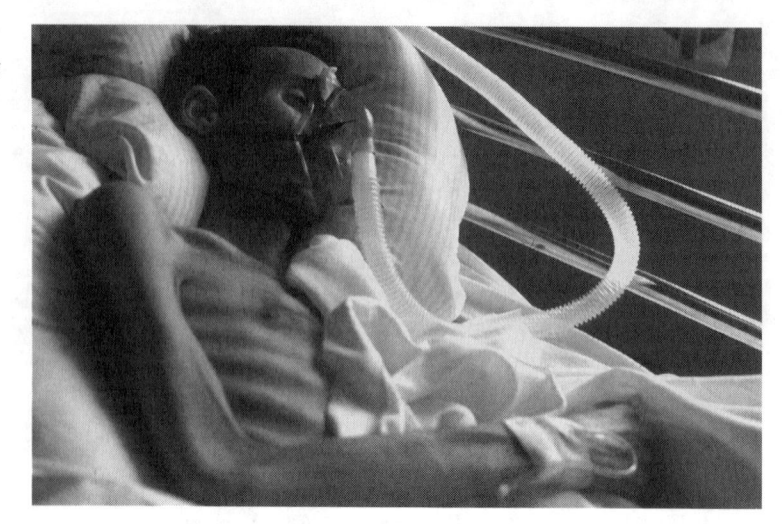

learned why, the terrible scourge of AIDS had claimed hundreds of lives and was well on its way to killing thousands more.

Deadly pneumonia strikes Los Angeles

The first documented cases of AIDS showed up in the world's major cities, Los Angeles among them. In Los Angeles between 1980 and 1981 doctors diagnosed five cases of an unusually severe pneumonia called *Pneumocystis carinii* pneumonia, or PCP. Caused by a common parasite, the microorganism *Pneumocystis carinii*, this form of pneumonia poses no problem for a person with a healthy immune system, which is the body's mechanism for fighting disease. But in a person with a damaged or compromised immune system—for example, a cancer patient receiving chemotherapy—PCP can kill. Usually, it doesn't. In typical cases, the pneumonia disappears as soon as treatment has restored the immune system.

But the PCP cases in Los Angeles were not typical. Intensive treatment had no effect on the conditions of the five men diagnosed with PCP. They all died well before doctors had a chance to learn the cause of their disease. The doctors puzzled over why these five patients (all previously healthy men between the ages of twenty-nine and thirty-six) had developed PCP. "None of these patients had an underlying disease that might have been associated with PCP or a history of treatment for a compromised immune system," write AIDS researchers Clyde B. McCoy and James A. Inciardi.[4]

Tests revealed that the patients had drastically reduced supplies of white blood cells, called T-helper cells or lymphocytes. The T-helper cells help run the human immune system by activating the body's disease-fighting mechanism and sending chemical messages for the creation of antibodies, which help to destroy harmful germs. In short, the patients' immune systems had stopped working for lack of T-helper cells, but no one knew what was killing off the T cells. Doctors in Los Angeles alerted their colleagues worldwide to the unexplained events occurring in their city.

A cautious warning

The first official announcement of the PCP outbreak in Los Angeles was published in June 1981 by the Centers for Disease Control (now called the Centers for Disease Control and Prevention) in Atlanta. The CDC, as it is commonly known, is the U.S. government's lead agency for tracking down disease outbreaks, or epidemics, and its bulletin *Morbidity and Mortality Weekly Report (MMWR)* is read by medical professionals worldwide. The June 5, 1981, issue described the five cases of PCP observed in Los Angeles between October 1980 and May 1981. Dr. Michael Gottlieb, an immune system specialist at UCLA Medical Center, and Dr. Wayne Shandera, of the Los Angeles County Department of Public Health, cautiously characterized the presence of PCP in five young, gay, and previously healthy men as "unusual." With little information to go on, they concluded that all the patients must have been exposed to something that had destroyed their immune systems. Without natural immunities, their bodies had not been able to fight off the parasite that causes PCP.

Although the article left more questions than answers, it served an important purpose. It alerted the medical community to a new and apparently deadly disease. "If this document was not the birth certificate of AIDS, it was cer-

Kaposi's sarcoma, a rare cancer appearing as blotches on the skin, was unknown to many doctors when the AIDS epidemic began.

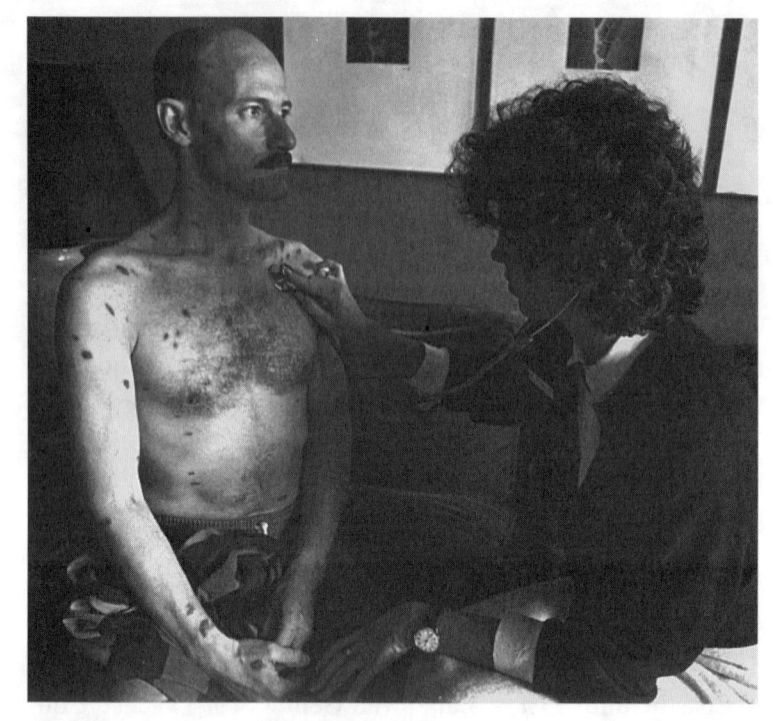

tainly the witness to its civil birth registration," writes physician and historian Mirko D. Grmek.[5]

A rare skin cancer in New York City

As the most populous city in the United States, New York could not escape the fast-developing epidemic. Between September 1979 and March 1981 doctors identified eight cases of a rare skin cancer called Kaposi's sarcoma (KS). Kaposi's sarcoma is a tumor of the blood vessel walls. It typically appears as blue-violet to brownish skin blotches. As cancers go, it is relatively benign. Its victims, mostly Mediterranean or Jewish men over the age of fifty, usually live for years after the disease shows up and often die of natural causes or other unrelated illnesses.

The patients diagnosed with KS in New York City between 1979 and 1981 did not fit the patient profile. All were young men and none were Jewish or of Mediterranean descent. What's more, their conditions were far from benign. As Grmek writes: "Their disorder was acutely malignant, departing from the traditional prognosis."[6] Their deaths came swiftly. Four of the eight had died by March 1981.

An unexplainable death

One of the first young KS patients to die was New York schoolteacher Rick Wellikoff. At the urging of a friend, Wellikoff had visited a dermatologist about some funny bumps behind his ear. The dermatologist sent Wellikoff to Dr. Linda Laubenstein for blood tests. Author and journalist Randy Shilts describes the doctor's visit:

> She duly noted the generalized rash that resisted treatment, and the enlarged lymph nodes all over his body. Laubenstein surveyed the man and assumed he had lymph cancer. Later a dermatologist told Linda [Laubenstein] that the man's rash was a skin cancer called Kaposi's sarcoma.[7]

Like a lot of other doctors, Laubenstein had never heard of Kaposi's sarcoma. Two weeks later, however, a colleague called to tell her that a second patient had been diagnosed with KS. Like Wellikoff, this man had none of the characteristics associated with KS. He was thirty-seven years old and neither Jewish nor of Mediterranean descent. Also like Wellikoff, he was gay.

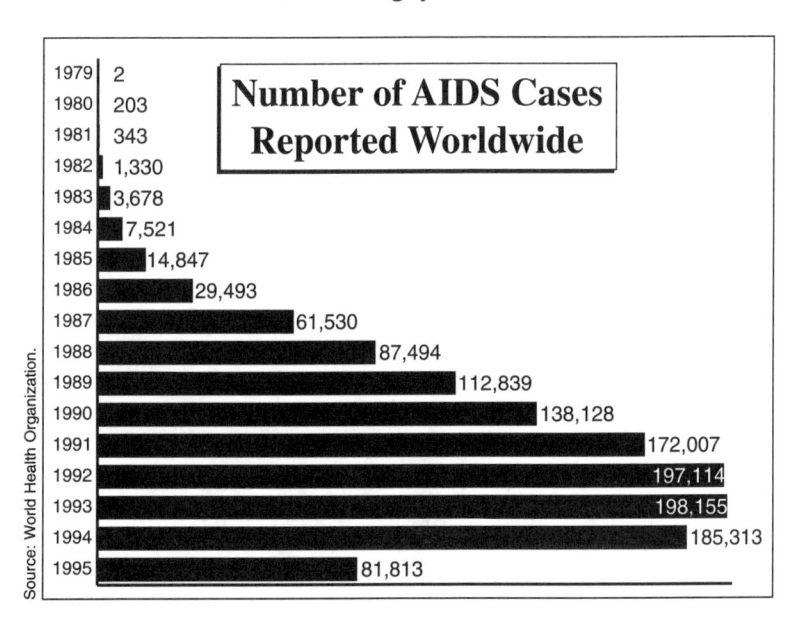

Number of AIDS Cases Reported Worldwide

Year	Cases
1979	2
1980	203
1981	343
1982	1,330
1983	3,678
1984	7,521
1985	14,847
1986	29,493
1987	61,530
1988	87,494
1989	112,839
1990	138,128
1991	172,007
1992	197,114
1993	198,155
1994	185,313
1995	81,813

Source: World Health Organization.

In just over a year Wellikoff's condition had worsened to the point of hopelessness. "Rick Wellikoff's rapid deterioration stunned his doctors no less than his friends. Kaposi's sarcoma wasn't supposed to act this way, Dr. Linda Laubenstein knew, but nonetheless Rick was dying," Shilts writes.[8]

By December 1980 Wellikoff's lungs had filled with a fluid that doctors could not identify. They told Wellikoff that they could continue to drain the fluid from his lungs and keep him alive with machines. On December 23 Wellikoff went home to die. Shilts describes the final night of Wellikoff's life:

> As the night wore on, Rick's lover sat at Rick's bedside and listened to his breaths grow shorter until, deep in the night, he stopped breathing altogether. In those first hours of the day . . . the thirty-seven-year-old fifth grade teacher passed away in a flat on West 78th Street, becoming the fourth American to die of what would later be called Acquired Immune Deficiency Syndrome.[9]

Like Rick Wellikoff, the early AIDS patients died without knowing what was killing them. They knew only that they had contracted rare conditions for which doctors had no explanation and no treatment.

Rumors

If AIDS patients knew little about their illnesses, the general public knew even less. Early reaction from members of the public—both gay and straight—was about the same: there simply was not much interest in a weird new disease supposedly attacking homosexual men. The *MMWR* article about *Pneumocystis carinii* pneumonia in Los Angeles attracted almost no attention from the mainstream media. An *MMWR* report a month later on PCP and Kaposi's sarcoma in New York City and California attracted more attention, with short stories appearing in major newspapers across the country. But media interest died quickly.

By this time, however, rumors of rare and deadly diseases attacking homosexuals had seeped into the nation's gay communities. Few took the rumors seriously. Many gays viewed the rumors as an attempt by the straight world to force gays to change their behavior. Some complained that media coverage, light as it was, provided just one more example of antigay bias in the press.

Gay media around the country did not respond much differently. They downplayed the reports of PCP and KS. Referring to the first *MMWR* article on PCP in Los Angeles, Shilts says, "Most gay papers across the country carried the item well off the front pages since it seemed, at best, to be some medical oddity that was probably blown out of proportion by homophobes in both the scientific establishment and the media."[10]

An indifferent, or in the case of the gay community, suspicious, public did not distract those members of the medical community who realized that something was very wrong. By the spring and summer of 1981 Kaposi's sarcoma and *Pneumocystis carinii* pneumonia had jumped to both coasts, with doctors in New York and California reporting twenty-six cases of KS by July. PCP had also spread, as had a number of other unusual conditions. These included toxoplasmosis, an infection of the brain caused by a parasite, and thrush, which is the growth in the throat of a fungus called *Candida*. Doctors describe all of these conditions as opportunistic infections because they rarely occur unless given a good opportunity such as a weakened immune system. Doctors soon realized that the presence of one or more opportunistic infections in an individual often signaled the onset of a rapid, unstoppable, ultimately fatal deterioration in a patient's health.

Tracking the disease

Doctors at the Centers for Disease Control were among the first to respond to the epidemic. The CDC convened a task force in June 1981 to find out whether a link existed between the outbreaks on both coasts and to try to understand what exactly was happening. Task force members included specialists in many fields of medicine, from immunology (the study of the immune system) to virology (the study of viruses). Together and separately they pursued any information that could shed light on the growing

Cases of PCP in heterosexual addicts confirmed researchers' suspicions that intravenous drug use could transmit the AIDS virus.

epidemic. They shared notes daily, fielded phone calls from doctors requesting information, and interviewed other health professionals who might have seen patients exhibiting signs of the still-unidentified disease. They scoured hospital records for possible unreported cases, and most importantly, tracked down and interviewed dozens of patients in hospital rooms and sickbeds across the country. The task force pursued its work "with a vigor that had earned the CDC the reputation as the world's foremost medical detective agency," Shilts says.[11]

Even before the release of the task force findings in mid-1982, some of the CDC doctors and a few of their colleagues outside the federal agency had drawn their own conclusions about the disease's cause and spread. By early 1982 at least two hundred cases of AIDS had been reported in fifteen states. Nearly all involved gay men who led active sex lives and lived in or had visited Los Angeles, New York City, or San Francisco, cities with large gay populations. Investigators also logged several cases of rapidly fatal PCP in heterosexuals. The only common characteristic of this group was intravenous drug use: all the patients, including one woman, were addicts.

These facts suggested similarities to another disease, hepatitis B, also common among gay men and intravenous drug users. Hepatitis B usually spreads to gay men through intimate sexual contact and to intravenous drug users through contaminated needles. This seemed a plausible explanation for the spread of the new disease. Some of the doctors even thought that the new disease, like hepatitis, might be caused by a virus. But the likeness to hepatitis B did not explain the damaged immune systems of infected patients, leaving a big gap in the theory that AIDS was due to a virus. Researchers pushed on, for they knew that only scientific proof would answer their many questions.

First real proof

Eventually, the proof came although not all at once. The first strong evidence to support the idea of sexual transmission emerged with the completion of the CDC study in June 1982. Investigators initially gathered information about the sexual partners of thirteen of the first nineteen AIDS patients; their subjects were homosexual men in Los Angeles. Within five years of developing their own symptoms, nine of the thirteen had had sexual contact with people who later developed Kaposi's sarcoma or *Pneumocystis carinii* pneumonia. Investigators then linked the records of those nine cases with another interconnected series of forty AIDS cases in ten different cities. Demonstrating the common thread in all of these instances of the disease was one individual who had developed Kaposi's sarcoma among other conditions. "Overall, the investigation of these 40 cases indicated that 20 percent of the initial AIDS cases in the United States were linked through sexual contact—a statistical clustering that was extremely unlikely to have occurred by chance," McCoy and Inciardi explain.[12] The significance of this finding was not lost on the researchers.

This was the evidence needed to support the theory of sexual transmission. But it still did not explain the number of heterosexual drug addicts who had also come down with the disease. None of them had had contact with any of the cluster studied by the CDC. Researchers suspected that they had contracted the disease from infected hypodermic needles. The sharing of needles is a sure route to passing on diseases carried in the blood because needles inserted in the veins allow the transport of blood particles from one person into the bloodstream of another. Knowing this to be so, researchers wondered about the risk of infection to the general public by blood and blood products.

Bad blood

"Confirmation was not long in coming," Grmek writes.[13] It came by way of the disease hemophilia, an inherited condition in which an individual—nearly always a man—lacks adequate quantities of the substance that enables blood to clot. To control bleeding, hemophiliacs inject themselves with a concentrated preparation made from the blood of human donors with normal clotting ability. Looking back, it is not surprising that AIDS showed up so quickly in people with hemophilia, since all hemophiliacs take these injections.

The CDC learned of the first case of an opportunistic infection in a person with hemophilia in January 1982. A Miami doctor reported that *Pneumocystis carinii* pneumonia had killed a hemophilia patient in his fifties. Two more cases were reported in July, and by the end of 1983, the CDC had recorded twenty-one American and eight European cases of infected hemophiliacs.

The hemophilia cases demonstrated that infection could spread through blood and blood products. But the absence of published reports of transmission by blood transfusion in patients who did not have hemophilia created some uncertainty. Surely, if the deadly disease was transmitted through blood and blood products, transfusions during surgeries would have resulted in more cases of the disease. Again, the proof was not long in coming. In November 1983 a Mayo Clinic medical team published a report of the case of a fifty-three-year-old man who had died of AIDS twenty-nine months after receiving a blood transfusion during open heart surgery. The man was not a hemophiliac, nor was he a drug addict or homosexual.

"The publication of the Mayo case . . . had the effect of a bombshell. An act of mercy, a triumph of modern medicine, had become a mortal menace," Grmek writes.[14] By the end of 1983, the CDC had logged thirty-nine cases in which a blood transfusion during the preceding five years appeared to be the only explanation for the onset of the disease.

More startling discoveries

The AIDS cases among hemophiliacs contributed to two other important discoveries. Until 1983, the possibility of the disease being passed between heterosexuals had not been reliably shown. By 1983, however, medical researchers were fairly certain that the disease could in fact be transmitted by heterosexuals as well as homosexuals. Reports of AIDS in companions of infected bisexuals and drug addicts provided some evidence. Stronger evidence surfaced in June 1983 when doctors diagnosed AIDS in the wife of a hemophiliac. Interviews with the couple confirmed the absence of all risk factors other than the man's hemophilia. With this information, "it became increasingly evident that AIDS was a sexually transmitted disease, and that 'sexual orientation' was not the element that placed people at risk," McCoy and Inciardi write.[15]

A serene 1985 family portrait belies the tragedy of a family destroyed by AIDS. The man contracted AIDS through treatment for hemophilia, then transmitted the disease to his wife, who infected their son at birth.

The other important discovery concerned the cause of AIDS. Although no known virus had ever carried out the destruction already attributed to the mysterious agent responsible for AIDS, many signs pointed to a virus. Doctors knew, for example, that viruses can quietly live in a person's body for years before causing illness. This property seemed to fit the profile of the AIDS-causing factor.

But the cause could not be established without hard evidence. That evidence came to light once AIDS had been diagnosed among hemophiliacs. The blood-clotting preparation used by hemophiliacs contains *filtered* blood products. The filtering process in use at the time removed potentially harmful bacteria, fungi, and protozoa but did not eliminate viruses, which are much smaller. "Since the infectious agent had obviously passed through a filter, it had to be a virus," Grmek writes.[16]

The search for the virus

Small groups of researchers in different corners of the world busied themselves with answering the question of which virus among the thousands of possible candidates causes AIDS. Scientists in the United States and France arrived at the answer in 1983 and 1984. Their discoveries ignited a dispute over who deserved credit for isolating the virus that causes AIDS. In the end, a world body of scientists agreed that credit would go to scientists from two respected institutions: the Pasteur Institute in Paris and the National Cancer Institute, which is part of the U.S. National Institutes of Health in Bethesda, Maryland.

The name given to the virus that causes AIDS is human immunodeficiency virus, or HIV. Like any virus, HIV can reproduce only inside the cells of a living host. As the virus multiplies, the healthy cells die and the host becomes ill. Illness does not necessarily occur right away, however. HIV can be present in the body for several years—usually between five and eight years—before obvious symptoms appear.

In the years following HIV's discovery, researchers have learned more about AIDS and about the virus that causes it. They know, for example, that HIV belongs to a group known as retroviruses. Retroviruses use a reverse chemical process from other viruses to achieve the same results, that is, duplication of themselves inside the cells of a host organism. However, HIV has a more complex structure than other viruses and even than other retroviruses. Bolstered by this complex structure, HIV's uniquely rapid reproductive abilities overwhelm the immune system and leave the body open to an array of opportunistic infections that frequently lead to death. For this reason, AIDS is often seen less as a single disease than as a "constellation of symptoms caused by infections and/or cancers, primarily due to disruption of the immune system by an underlying viral infection," authors Paul Harding Douglas and Laura Pinsky write.[17]

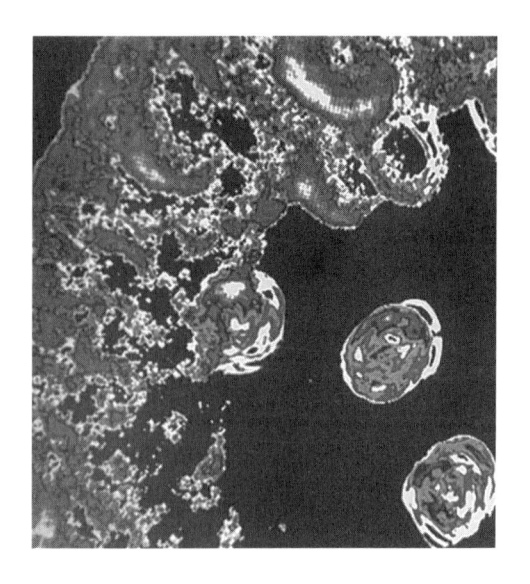

Just as researchers now know more about the virus itself, they also know a great deal more about how it spreads. Transmission of HIV takes place when virus particles or infected cells gain direct access to the bloodstream. This can occur through sexual intercourse, through the sharing of contaminated needles, through blood and blood products, and in the womb, where a fetus can acquire the virus from an infected mother. HIV is not spread by air, by dirty objects, by ingestion, or by casual contact with an infected person. As Grmek writes:

A microscopic view of HIV, the microorganism that destroys the immune system and leaves the body vulnerable to other infections.

> There is absolutely no evidence that AIDS has ever been spread under normal living conditions—not in schools, not in crowded buses or trains, not in restaurants, not at the hairdressers', not in business meetings, not even between members of the same family who live in abject poverty and share the most dismal of sanitary conditions. AIDS cannot be contracted from a handshake, a swimming pool, or toilet seat. It breaks through the barrier separating individuals only by sexual activity, the biology of maternity, the injection of drugs, or medical intervention.[18]

Doctors, medical researchers, and the general public have learned a great deal about AIDS since the first cases surfaced almost twenty years ago. A great deal more has yet to be uncovered as AIDS continues its death march through humanity.

2
The Challenge of Preventing AIDS

WITH GREAT FANFARE, federal public health officials announced in 1997 that prevention efforts were finally paying off, for AIDS deaths had started to decline. At the same time, however, they noted that at least forty thousand new HIV infections occur in the United States every year. A small percentage of these infections are present at birth or occur through blood transfusions. However, the vast majority of people who contract the AIDS virus do so by engaging in risky behavior. Sixty percent of the 476,899 AIDS cases reported to the Centers for Disease Control as of June 1995 resulted from sexual contact. Thirty-two percent resulted from shared needles. These numbers illustrate the difficulty of preventing an infectious disease that is, as one group of researchers states, "largely a disease of behaviors."[19]

Without a preventive vaccine, and with little hope of seeing one soon, prevention depends largely on individuals changing their behavior and on public support for programs that encourage such change. As one group of AIDS researchers writes in the *Journal of the American Medical Association (JAMA):*

> Because AIDS is largely a disease of behaviors, confronting the AIDS epidemic will require an unwavering commitment to prevention efforts to change behavior. The first decade of the epidemic has taught us that lasting changes in behavior needed to avoid infection can occur as a result of carefully tailored, targeted, and persistent prevention efforts.[20]

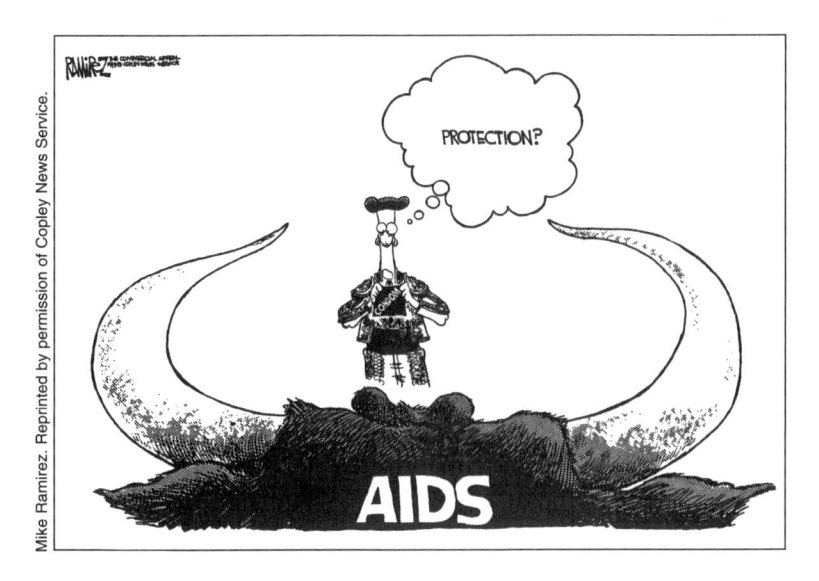

However, because human behavior is not always predictable and because human beings are not always rational, the prevention of AIDS presents a formidable challenge.

Human nature complicates prevention

For one thing, people don't always tell the truth about themselves. Some people who know they're infected with HIV don't tell sexual partners about their condition out of fear of rejection (or even out of meanness). The more common situation probably involves individuals who have exposed themselves to possible infection through their behavior but haven't been tested for HIV and allow concerns about harming new relationships to prevent them from warning their sexual partners. William H. Masters, Virginia E. Johnson, and Robert C. Kolodny, known for their pioneering research in the area of human sexuality, make this point when they write, "It is not difficult to imagine circumstances in which revealing one's sexual history to a partner could precipitate the breakup of a relationship, or at least seriously undermine the trust of that relationship."[21] Human nature, and the sometimes troubled relationships between men and women, complicate prevention efforts in other ways, too.

Even when people have the tools for protecting themselves from HIV infection, they don't always use them. Condoms have long been promoted as a means of reducing the risk of infection during sexual intercourse. But many women have difficulty asking their sexual partners to use condoms. Some men don't like condoms and become irate when asked to use them. So, many women just don't ask, or they ask but don't force the issue if they get a negative response.

People continue to have unprotected sex even though they know that condoms reduce the risk of transmitting AIDS through sexual intercourse.

These and other aspects of human nature have been blamed in part for the rise in the number of women with AIDS. According to the Centers for Disease Control, women account for about 13 percent of all AIDS cases reported in the United States so far. However, the proportion of cases among women has steadily increased over the last ten years. Between July 1994 and June 1995 alone, women represented 18 percent of new AIDS cases. CDC studies show that 36 percent of the 64,822 women with AIDS as of June 1995 were infected through sexual contact. "Women nationally are the most rapidly growing group of HIV infections," says Dr. Ruth Greenblatt, director of the Women's Specialty Center at the University of California-San Francisco Medical Center.[22] Greenblatt says that women are more likely to be at risk from the behavior of others than from their own behavior.

Reducing the risks

Experts realize that people often have difficulty changing their habits, especially those that bring immediate or pleasurable results, and especially when negative consequences may be years away. For this reason, many AIDS prevention efforts focus on promoting small changes in behavior. While small changes won't eliminate the risk of contracting HIV, they can reduce that risk. For example, many public health campaigns urge use of condoms during sex rather than suggesting that people abstain from sexual relations. Other programs encourage drug addicts to exchange used needles for sterile ones instead of trying to get people to give up drugs. This method of prevention is called risk reduction, and it is a source of controversy in many areas of AIDS prevention.

The primary concern about risk reduction is that it does not require (or help) the individual to change irresponsible or harmful behavior. For example, the drug addict may lessen the risk of HIV infection by using clean needles but he or she is still injecting dangerous drugs. "Keeping people addicted, albeit with clean needles, merely shifts the location of risk," writes Bonnie Shullenberger, a former New York hospital chaplain who worked with AIDS patients.[23]

However, risk reduction is a common strategy of people trying to reduce the destructive effects of drug abuse. Those who work in that field say it is impossible to get all drug users to stop using drugs. Instead, they strive to lessen the harm drug addicts might do to themselves (and others) as a result of their habit.

People who risk death every day

Researchers generally agree that it is difficult to change the behavior of intravenous drug users because their lifestyle frequently puts them at risk of death. Writers McCoy and Inciardi, who believe that people who expose themselves to violence, sickness, and death almost every day are unlikely to change behavior that might cause sickness and death a few years in the future, quote one prostitute, a user of intravenous cocaine:

This young man and woman died of AIDS within six months of each other. Behavior change is an essential part of AIDS prevention efforts.

> Every day I risk my health, and my life for that matter, when I shoot up. Every time I go out to cop [buy drugs] I risk getting cut [stabbed] or even killed. Every time I'm strolling [walking the streets soliciting clients] at night, there are all kinds of crazies, geeks, thugs . . . out there. Now they say that if I use some dirty needle I can get sick, even die in a few years. So I care? I'm probably already dead. Why should I care?[24]

Despite the difficulties, promoting behavior change among users of intravenous (IV) drugs—drugs that are injected into the veins—is important in slowing the spread of HIV. Recent studies show that one-third of all people with AIDS in the United States probably contracted HIV through needle sharing or through sexual relations with an infected intravenous drug user. Studies also show that 60 percent of American children with AIDS were infected through the birth process by a drug-using, HIV-positive mother. Many experts support prevention efforts that combine drug treatment, face-to-face counseling from former IV drug users, teaching of needle-cleaning methods and condom use, and programs that allow IV drug users to exchange used needles for wrapped, sterile units. Of those approaches, needle exchange programs have prompted the most controversy.

Concerns about needle exchanges

Needle exchange programs have a simple goal: to reduce the spread of HIV by removing contaminated needles and syringes from circulation. However, efforts to run needle exchanges have been anything but simple. Congress banned the use of federal funds for needle exchange programs in the late 1980s. Supporters of the ban feared that government sponsorship would give people the idea that

> **Cutting the Risk**
>
> - Number of intravenous drug users in U.S. large metropolitan areas: 1,460,300
>
> - Number HIV positive: 204,000 or 14%
>
> - Estimated new HIV infections among intravenous drug users: 19,000/year
>
> - HIV infections potentially averted through implementing needle exchange programs:
>
> | | |
> |---|---|
> | 1987 to 1995 | 4,394–9,666 |
> | 1996 to 2000 | 5,150–11,329 |

Source: Peter Lurie and Ernest Drucker, *Wall Street Journal*, July 10, 1996.

drug-using behavior is acceptable. They also worried that such programs would increase the number of drug users by making drug paraphernalia easily available to addicts. Some, like former hospital chaplain Bonnie Shullenberger, doubt that needle exchanges will slow the spread of AIDS—with or without government help:

> On the surface, it looks easy: give addicts clean syringes, and they won't pass a needle around, which means they won't spread the virus. This assumes, of course, that junkies are careful, conscientious people (like us) who will naturally be grateful for this kindly assist in health management. However ... an addict has three states of life: stoned, searching, and sick. A person with a moderate habit might use a personal needle if he scores in a not-too-desperate searching state. A broke, severely addicted person who's in a sick state isn't capable of caution.... That's when ... clean-needle programs are about as meaningful as dust.[25]

Concerns and objections such as these have kept the federal government from lifting the ban and have blocked efforts to start or continue needle exchanges in some cities.

Studies show that needle exchanges work

As of 1995, more than seventy needle exchange programs operated in fifty-five U.S. cities, but without federal funding. Recent studies of some of those programs, and of similar

Marchers demonstrate their support for needle distribution programs as a means of slowing the spread of AIDS.

programs in other countries, show that needle exchanges can reduce the spread of HIV. Two studies, one by the CDC and another by a panel of experts selected by the National Institutes of Health (NIH), are especially noteworthy.

In the CDC study, completed in September 1993, investigators looked at existing research on the topic, visited twenty-three needle exchange programs in fifteen cities in four different countries, and surveyed reports of other U.S. programs that were not visited. The study showed that needle exchange programs are effective in reducing HIV infection yet do not encourage illegal drug use, says its principal investigator.

The NIH panel announced the results of its study in February 1997. The panel found that needle exchange programs in New Haven, Connecticut, and in the Dutch city of Amsterdam did not lead to increased drug use, encourage young people to start using drugs, or result in more needles being discarded in public places. The NIH panel concluded that such programs reduce needle sharing among drug users by 80 percent, which translates to an estimated 30 percent decrease in new HIV infections.

Studies such as these have prompted calls for lifting the federal ban on funding for needle exchange programs. Even if the ban is lifted, controversy about how to prevent the spread of AIDS is likely to continue—especially in the area of education.

The importance of education

Most people agree that education is a necessary part of any prevention effort. There is disagreement, however, on the content of the information provided (whether to focus on changing overall behavior or on reducing risks), and on who should be given this information, and at what age. One of the areas of greatest controversy concerns children and adolescents.

Young people are turning up with HIV in greater numbers than ever before. The White House Office on National AIDS Policy reports that people younger than twenty-one account for one in four new infections, and half of all new infections are among people under twenty-five. Additionally, according to the Center for Population Options, one out of every five individuals with AIDS is believed to have contracted HIV as a teenager. These statistics add to concerns about what young people are learning about HIV and AIDS and when and how they learn it.

AIDS education for young people, regardless of content or method, always encounters one obstacle: the nature of youth. Adolescence is a time of exploration and development, and taking risks is a normal part of both. "Kids think they're invincible," says one California AIDS worker.[26] To illustrate, she recalled a conversation with a woman who was concerned about her niece: the girl said she did not worry about AIDS because she assumed that by the time she got it, there would be a cure. The aunt took this to mean that her niece felt free to experiment with sex without heeding warnings about HIV and AIDS.

Adolescence is also a time of passion. Young people have strong passions, and sexual experimentation is one expression of those passions. When passion and a sense of

Drug users receive syringes, bleach, and other equipment as part of a controversial AIDS prevention effort.

immortality combine with the growing desire for independence, good judgment does not always prevail. Young people sometimes have difficulty recognizing that their actions today may have serious—and possibly deadly—consequences tomorrow. The challenge of AIDS education is finding a way to overcome these attitudes. "Unless adolescents and young adults can be convinced that the AIDS virus is a reality in their world right now, it is unlikely that there will be enough of a shift in behavior to keep this epidemic from expanding at an alarming rate," say Masters, Johnson, and Kolodny.[27]

The question of how to get young people to think realistically about AIDS is the subject of much debate. Most AIDS education programs for youth fall into one of two categories: those that urge abstinence from sex until adulthood (when sexual activity should be restricted to a faithful, monogamous relationship) and those that discuss safe sex practices, especially use of condoms. Both approaches have numerous supporters—and critics.

Teaching abstinence

Abstinence-only educational programs teach kids that there is value in not having sex until adulthood, and then with only one partner. This approach builds on the view that young people are not emotionally mature enough to have sex. Perhaps the best support for this view comes in the form of teenage pregnancy statistics. The United States has one of the highest teen pregnancy rates in the industrialized world. From these statistics, the question arises: If young people aren't mature enough to use contraceptives to prevent pregnancy, is it reasonable to expect them to be mature enough to protect themselves from AIDS?

Currently, the most effective method of AIDS protection during sex is the condom. But condoms are not fail-safe devices; they don't always work. "When used for contraception, they fail as much as 10 to 15 percent of the time. Some studies suggest they are even less effective in preventing infection with sexually transmitted diseases, including HIV, which can occur more easily than impregnation," Ken Sidey, associate editor of the magazine *Christianity Today*, writes.[28]

Defects, breakage, and improper use all can render condoms ineffective. Given the failure rate of condoms, Sidey and others say, the safe sex message is misleading. "What does work—all the time—is abstinence," Sidey writes.[29] And this is the course Sidey and others propose for young people until they reach adulthood and until they are ready to restrict sexual activity to a faithful, monogamous relationship.

Another concern is the possibility that young people will misinterpret what they learn. Many people are troubled by the idea that teenagers might get the impression from AIDS education programs that sex is okay at any age as long as the individuals take precautions. *Child and Family* magazine editor Herbert Ratner expresses this concern:

> Those who stress condom usage only put the seal of approval on active genital sex. The message it communicates is that the condom is a good which converts irresponsible sex into responsible sex, giving it the appearance of acceptability and respectability.[30]

AIDS prevention efforts would be furthered, Ratner believes, not by teaching young people how to have sex safely but by teaching them the value of abstinence while they are young and monogamy when they are older.

Teaching safe sex

Many critics of the abstinence-only approach agree that immature adolescents should postpone their introduction to sexual relations. But they also believe that many young people will not wait, and without information about how to protect themselves, members of this group will be vulnerable to HIV infection. For this reason, they urge candid discussion of sexuality, both heterosexual and homosexual, and the safe sex practices that can help prevent HIV infection. (Such programs usually also include discussion of drug use.)

To be effective, supporters of this approach say, programs must be explicit. They must "create a sense of emergency about AIDS among adolescents in order to help break through their enormous denial about their risk for HIV," an advisory council to the New York City schools stated a few years ago.[31] Some of the most innovative AIDS education programs combine frank discussion in the classroom with visits from young men and women who have AIDS or are HIV-positive. But these programs are a rarity.

Outreach workers hand out information on AIDS, safe sex, and condoms to young women. Critics say such efforts encourage young people to have sex prematurely.

Although most states require some form of AIDS education in the public schools, political and parental pressures have weakened many of the programs, one writer contends. Some are not even allowed to mention condoms in their discussions. "Most of these programs give out plenty of information about AIDS but do virtually nothing to show teenagers how to practice safe sex or to abstain," says Debra Haffner, of the New York–based Sex Information and Education Council. She continues:

[The programs] need to tell teenagers *how* to say no when someone is pressuring them into having sex and how to avoid potentially dangerous situations. They need to show teenagers how to use condoms and where to buy them—or even give them out for free. The underlying problem is that as a nation we are unwilling to acknowledge our teenagers as sexual beings. But until we start being more honest, lots of young people will die.[32]

When to present this information to young people poses another problem for parents, educators, and politicians.

At what age should AIDS education begin?

Most AIDS education programs focus their efforts on adolescents. However, some programs target much younger children. One school official in Washington, D.C., supports programs for children of preschool age. Young children, she says, need to be warned against picking up or playing with needles or other drug paraphernalia they might find on the ground. Some teachers even warn second graders against the ancient childhood rite of pricking each other's fingers in "blood brothers" ceremonies.

Many AIDS researchers recommend that AIDS education begin early, although perhaps not as early as preschool or second grade. Timing is critical, one group of researchers states. Programs that begin before young people have become sexually active or had a chance to use drugs have been more successful than programs begun after many teens have had these experiences. Researchers such as Masters, Johnson, and Kolodny urge public schools to begin AIDS education by the fourth or fifth grade, tailoring the complexity of the information to the age group. "While the level of sophistication will obviously deepen with older students, repeated reinforcement of the prevention message at each grade level is necessary" to make the effort worthwhile, they write.[33]

People need more than facts

Experts recommend that AIDS education reach beyond the public schools—to colleges and universities, to groups that practice high-risk behavior, and to the general public. However, experience has shown that education must do more than provide facts. Some of the earliest prevention efforts revolved around public awareness campaigns. In 1988, for example, the U.S. Department of Health and Human Services mailed an eight-page brochure entitled *Understanding AIDS* to every household in the country. Studies have found little evidence of behavior change in response to public education campaigns such as this one. Among the reasons, McCoy and Inciardi suggest, is that "people may understand and learn what public health professionals want them to know, but they may not consider the information to be personally relevant to them. They may not see themselves at risk, or they may not feel that they are capable of modifying the behaviors that place them at risk."[34]

For education to have any real effect, it must bring about lasting change. Researchers Masters, Johnson, and Kolodny offer this view of education's role in AIDS prevention efforts:

> Unless education results in concrete changes in sexual behavior and meaningful reduction in the sharing of contaminated needles and syringes, it is unlikely to serve a useful public health function. To produce these sorts of changes, education must motivate as well as inform.[35]

Most experts would agree with this view, adding only that education cannot help bring about lasting change unless other prevention efforts are set in motion as well.

3

Testing for HIV Infection

MARCH 2, 1985, MARKED A turning point in the AIDS epidemic. On that date, Irwin Memorial Blood Bank in San Francisco received a shipment of HIV antibody tests, the first such tests to be publicly released in the United States. Within days, blood banks and plasma centers nationwide had received their test kits. The test could not detect AIDS or even the presence of the AIDS virus. What the test could do is indicate the presence of HIV antibodies, which are the one sure sign of HIV infection. Today's tests perform the same function.

The antibody test represented an important breakthrough in the slow-moving search for ways to protect the public from the devastating AIDS virus. Author and journalist Randy Shilts explains its significance:

> From now on, the chances of contracting AIDS through blood transfusion were effectively eliminated or, at last, were truthfully reduced to one in a million. That much was simple, but it was probably the only simple aspect of the enormous implications that the beige plastic test kits held for the future of the AIDS epidemic in general and the gay community in particular.[36]

As it turns out, the antibody test also had broad implications for segments of the population outside the gay community.

The antibody test used to screen donated blood in blood banks can also be used to determine whether an individual has been infected with the AIDS virus. It has been used voluntarily for this purpose by thousands of people nationwide, and it is used routinely to screen American military personnel, U.S. foreign service employees, federal prison inmates, and immigrants entering the United States. But, other than in blood banks, the test has not been used in the general population in any organized way nationwide. The same is true of other public health measures traditionally used to stop the spread of infectious and sexually transmitted diseases.

Objections to the absence of standard public health measures in the face of so devastating a disease have been raised over the years, as have concerns about the potential for violating an individual's privacy and leaving that person open to discrimination on the job, in housing, in health insurance, and in medical care. The HIV testing issue is once again at the forefront of the AIDS debate. The discussion is fueled this time by new research and statistics. New research demonstrates the benefits of early treatment for people infected with HIV and of prenatal treatment for the babies of HIV-infected women. New statistics show that although fewer people are dying each year from AIDS (thanks largely to new drugs and ongoing prevention efforts), the rate of HIV infection is rising in some segments of the population, particularly among women, blacks, and Hispanics.

The testing debate is as bitter as any that has ever coursed through the public health arena. Some describe it as a conflict between individual civil rights and overall public health, a view reflected by Helen Mathews Smith, former editor of *MD* magazine:

> For more than a decade, bowing to narrow interests, American public health officials have ignored the central tenets of plague control: routine testing, tracking the path of the disease, and warnings to those at risk. . . . In the end, the medical establishment voted for individual rights over public health.[37]

Others portray the debate over testing as a charade in which one segment of society pretends concern about another, with the real aim being to force people to live their lives according to one set of rules. "Social control in the name of public health has a long . . . history in this country," writes AIDS activist Sandor Katz. The real focus of calls for mandatory testing and other measures, Katz writes, is "identification of the infected rather than care and prevention."[38]

As divisive as the debate over testing has become, most people agree that HIV testing is essential—both for prevention and treatment. Those who do not know they are infected will not seek treatment and will not take precautions to avoid spreading the infection to others. Ultimately, then, the debate is not about the importance of testing but about how and when to conduct HIV testing, and whom to test, and what to do with the results.

Navy personnel, discharged after testing positive for HIV, serve as examples for members of the public who fear the effect of routine HIV testing.

Standard practice

Public health authorities have followed standard measures for controlling infectious and sexually transmitted diseases since well before the United States recorded its first cases of AIDS. These measures include routine testing (that is, using a test that can be done as a matter of course without specific permission from the patient); reporting (providing the names of those who test positive for infection to local health departments); contact tracing (identifying people who might have been exposed to infection); and notification (finding and informing all those whose names turned up during contact tracing). Although public health records contain the names of these who test positive for infection, those names are strictly confidential. Public health workers generally believe that they have more control over the follow-up process when they have names. However, they do not reveal any names even during the contact tracing and notification processes.

The standard measures just described have effectively controlled outbreaks of infectious diseases such as typhoid, diphtheria, and tuberculosis, and upsurges in sexually transmitted diseases such as syphilis. In the 1930s, for example, the U.S. surgeon general instituted an aggressive testing and partner notification program to combat an outbreak of the sexually transmitted disease syphilis. Untreated, syphilis can be incapacitating and even fatal; although it is primarily spread through sexual contact, it can also be passed on at birth. The standard treatment for syphilis today, the antibiotic penicillin, had not been discovered in the 1930s. Even so, the testing and notification effort brought the infant and adult epidemic under control.

Despite the success of this and other organized public health campaigns, there has been no coordinated, national response to HIV and AIDS. "Although various traditional public-health steps are being taken against AIDS and HIV, in differing combination from state to state, the result is a chaotic patchwork—one that is inadequate, a growing number of critics say, to the task of containing and eradicating AIDS," author Chandler Burr writes.[39]

Fear of discrimination

The origins of this public health response can be found in the earliest days of the AIDS epidemic. When AIDS first appeared in the United States, it took its greatest toll among gay men. Both within and outside the gay community, it came to be regarded as a "gay disease." And because doctors knew of no cure or treatment, a test that could identify those infected with the AIDS virus seemed to many in the gay community to be just another way of identifying and persecuting gays. "With as many as one-half of gay men testing positive for [HIV] in some studies, it appeared that the test could well become a de facto test for sexual orientation," writes author and journalist Randy Shilts.[40]

Rumors of mass quarantines of AIDS-infected gays and of the HIV test being used as a condition for employment or insurance coverage swirled through the gay community. Although such fears may have been exaggerated, they were not altogether baseless. In February 1985, for example (about two weeks before the tests became available), a Florida health department official told representatives of the CDC and the U.S. Food and Drug Administration that he "already had been contacted by school districts eager to weed out gay teachers and by country clubs who wanted to use the test to screen food handlers."[41]

The fear of being publicly exposed as homosexual was compounded by the fear of being identified as infected with the deadly AIDS virus. As author and journalist Elinor Burkett states:

> In the first months and years of the epidemic people with AIDS died in the hallways of hospitals, where nurses wouldn't touch them. They were kicked out of their apartments.

A 1986 photo illustrates one source of concern for the gay community, which feared AIDS testing would lead to quarantines and worse.

Insurance companies canceled their policies. Their bosses fired them. They had no idea how to get Social Security disability payments or Medicaid.[42]

An environment clouded by fear threatened any real chance of cooperation between public health officials and the gay community. This, in turn, threatened the effort to learn more about AIDS and how it spread. "Public-health authorities, faced with a fatal, communicable disease whose method of transmission they did not understand, desperately needed the cooperation of the infected—as they would in any epidemic," writes Chandler Burr.[43]

A broader public health question

To obtain that cooperation, CDC officials guaranteed gay leaders that all tests would be voluntary, and all results confidential and anonymous. Confidentiality had long been standard in public health disease control efforts. This time, however, testing would be voluntary and anonymous. Test results would be used only for blood bank screening and research, not to identify infected individuals. Contact tracing and partner notification would be done only if a person who tested positive for infection asked for help in contacting others who might have been exposed. While this agreement helped assure the gay community that the government would not use test results to publicly identify male homosexuals, Randy Shilts writes, it did not address "the broader public health question of how you can control a disease if you decline to find out who is infected."[44]

Although in all fifty states confirmed cases of AIDS are reported to public health departments (with individual names held in confidence), the CDC still adheres to the rules it set down in the 1980s—its HIV tests are done on a voluntary basis and results remain anonymous. Every blood sample the CDC tests for HIV is identified by a number which is used instead of the person's name in all agency records and reports; thus someone who wants to learn his or her test results can ask for them by number, but no one who examines the records will be able to identify this individual, or any other. A person who tests positive can ask trained health department counselors to notify partners for him or her. However, health workers do not routinely set out to track down and inform all people who may have been exposed to the AIDS virus (as they do for other infectious and sexually transmitted diseases). In some cases, health workers are even barred from notifying spouses of HIV-positive individuals that they are at grave risk of infection. Author Chandler Burr believes that efforts to address civil rights concerns have badly hampered efforts to halt the spread of HIV and AIDS:

> The result, ultimately, was the effective suspension of traditional public-health procedures for AIDS, which is to say, there would be no routine testing for HIV; the reporting of the names of the HIV-infected would be required only in some places, and would miss the epidemic's hotspots; and contact tracing and notification would as a result be greatly handicapped, and in many places pursued in desultory fashion if at all, often in the face of opposition. All efforts were to be voluntary—dependent on educational outreach and persuasion rather than on systematic procedures.[45]

Not all states have followed the CDC's lead in adopting voluntary and anonymous testing programs. Colorado and Minnesota began routine HIV testing and name reporting in the mid-1980s. At least twenty-six states now require reporting by name (to local and state health departments) for anyone who tests positive for HIV infection. Thirty-three states have adopted laws that allow doctors or public health workers to notify sex or needle-sharing partners of those who test positive for the AIDS virus. However, the two states with the highest rates of HIV infection, New York and California, have no broad reporting requirements for HIV. In these states, as in some others, education and counseling are stressed over mandatory testing and name reporting.

The power of education and persuasion

While criticized by some, reliance on education and persuasion has won many supporters. Adherents of this approach view education and counseling as more persuasive than laws that try to mandate behavior. For regardless of the laws, testing, name reporting, and contact tracing can be done only with the cooperation of individuals. Dr. Helene D. Gayle of the CDC makes this point when she writes:

> Protecting the public health requires voluntary individual commitment as well as sound public leadership. This is as true for preventing HIV as it is for preventing other infectious disease. People have to come in for testing, provide their contacts' names, comply with complex treatment options, and change behavior to prevent the spread of infection. Historically, approaching individuals in an atmosphere of cooperation and trust has worked better. We can't mandate HIV away. It's just not that simple.[46]

Opponents of mandatory HIV testing and name reporting believe that these actions will scare people away from being tested.

The idea that mandatory testing and name reporting will scare people away from getting tested is central to arguments in favor of education. A frequently cited study in support of this view was presented in 1988 at the Fourth Annual Conference on AIDS in Stockholm, Sweden. Researchers at the University of South Carolina charted changes in HIV testing patterns after South Carolina switched from anonymous testing to mandatory name reporting in 1986. Researchers found a 51 percent drop in the number of gay men tested but a slight increase in the total number of people tested. Among those tested, however, positive results decreased by 43 percent. "The study demonstrates that ending anonymous testing and requiring the reporting of names serve to scare away from diagnostic information and health care those people at greatest risk," writes AIDS activist Sandor Katz.[47]

While the belief that all AIDS testing should be anonymous still has many supporters, an increasing number of people are beginning to question the "exceptional public-health status of AIDS," as one writer calls it.[48] In March 1997, Congressman Tom Coburn of Oklahoma introduced a bill to establish confidential HIV reporting nationwide and to make states responsible for notifying anyone who has been exposed to HIV. Coburn's bill, called the HIV Prevention Act of 1997, was expected to be scheduled for hearings in early 1998.

Other legislation, including a bill enacted by Congress in 1996, targets testing and notification issues relating to pregnant women and newborn infants. The debate on these issues is as polarized as the other testing-related issues. New and proposed laws have done little to calm the emotional tone of the discussion.

Counseling pregnant women

At the heart of this debate is new research that demonstrates the benefits of early treatment for HIV-positive individuals and for the babies of HIV-infected women. New drugs called protease inhibitors, given in combination with other drugs, have shown a remarkable ability to prolong the lives of people infected with the AIDS virus, especially when given immediately after infection. Recent research also shows that the drug AZT, given to an HIV-positive woman during pregnancy and delivery, can prevent transmission of the virus to the baby. Without treatment, about 25 percent of the fetuses of HIV-infected mothers are also infected. With treatment, that number decreases to about 8 percent. Treatment after the baby is born can improve the quality of life for that baby but, so far at least, cannot eliminate the virus.

Approximately seven thousand HIV-infected women give birth in the United States each year. However, few doctors or clinics today routinely test pregnant women for the AIDS virus. More often, pregnant women are counseled, meaning that doctors, nurses, or other health workers discuss the HIV test and urge patients, especially

A foster mother cares for a baby with AIDS. Drugs can prevent transmission of HIV from mother to fetus and prolong the life of HIV-positive babies, but doctors do not routinely test pregnant women for the virus.

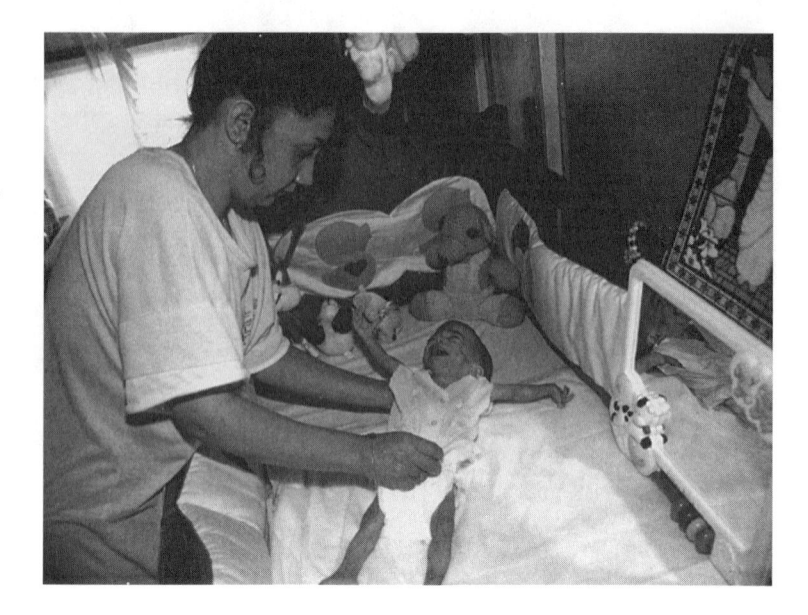

women considered to be in a high-risk group, to be tested. Researchers have found that private practitioners do not routinely do such counseling because patients who can afford medical coverage (or who have coverage provided by an employer) are often seen as having less risk for HIV infection. In most cases, the HIV test is given only to women who consent explicitly (often in writing) to the test and state that they are willing to learn the results.

Counseling and voluntary testing can be effective. Harlem Hospital in New York is often cited as an example of a successful program. "Its intensive and closely supervised counseling program is successful in persuading 90 percent of pregnant women or new mothers to be tested or to have their infants tested," a team of writers reports in *State Legislatures* magazine.[49]

However, voluntary testing and counseling often do not succeed. Doctors at Metropolitan Hospital in East Harlem, New York, believe that 60 to 70 percent of HIV-infected pregnant women are never identified by the hospital despite counseling that urges them to take the test. "Women refuse the test because they don't believe they are at risk or because they are afraid of the test results," say the *State Legislatures* writers.[50]

Newborn testing

Although few states routinely test pregnant women for HIV, forty-four states routinely test newborn infants for the presence of HIV antibodies. Test results are used exclusively for monitoring infection rates. They are not given to the parents (or the doctor) even if the baby tests positive for HIV infection. The reason is found in the belief that routine infant testing infringes on the mother's rights. As one AIDS program manager explains:

> Infant testing doesn't test infants; it tests mothers. All children of HIV-positive mothers test positive at birth, but less than 25% of them are still positive after 18 months. Revealing the HIV status of these infants, whose mothers never agreed to testing or disclosure, would violate the mother's right to informed consent.[51]

This set of circumstances troubles many people, both in and out of the health care field.

One member of the New York State Assembly tried to remedy the situation in her state by introducing a bill that would have required health authorities to share test results with the mothers of HIV-positive infants and their doctors. The bill's sponsor, Nettie Mayersohn, believes that the baby's life is more valuable than the mother's right to privacy. "Countless people tell me that I will be destroying the mother's privacy and also that she has the right not to know," Mayersohn says. "They completely dismiss the fact that there is now another human life involved whose right to medical care—and indeed to life—is being violated."[52]

Opposition to this bill, and to similar legislation introduced in the U.S. Congress in 1995, was fierce. Opponents pointed out that revealing the names of infants who tested positive for HIV infection would not protect the infants, since transmission had already occurred, but stated their belief that it would violate the privacy of the mothers. They also argued that many women would be so frightened by the prospect of being identified by name as infected with HIV that they might avoid prenatal care altogether.

The New York State Assembly killed Mayersohn's bill in 1994. The 1995 congressional bill, called the Newborn

Infant HIV Notification Act, was withdrawn after the CDC halted its newborn testing program to protest the bill's mandatory notification provision. The bill's sponsor, Congressman Gary Ackerman of New York, joined Oklahoma's Tom Coburn in drafting new legislation. That legislation, enacted in 1996, requires state health care workers to offer counseling and voluntary testing to pregnant women who have not been tested for HIV. The legislation also sets goals for voluntary HIV testing of pregnant women and reducing HIV infection rates in infants. States that fail to meet those goals by the year 2000 will have to begin mandatory infant testing or lose federal AIDS funding.

Mandatory infant testing and disclosure begins in New York

Recently, New York legislators changed their views on infant testing. In February 1997, New York became the first state in the nation to require HIV testing and disclosure of test results for all newborns. Under New York law, mothers and doctors must be told whether a newborn infant tests positive for HIV infection. The biggest problems so far seem to be logistical. Hospitals, for example, usually record test results for newborns and other patients on computers. But strict rules on confidentiality mean that this information is generally not included in computer records, so hospitals have to find other ways to store HIV test results.

Reactions from patients vary. In New York City, one new mother interviewed at Bellevue Hospital Center's maternity ward had taken a prenatal HIV test at a clinic and tested negative. "I think the testing is very, very important because the baby's health is more important than the mother's feelings," said twenty-five-year-old Mabel Buritica.[53] Another woman, one week away from delivery, was interviewed while waiting for a friend in the maternity ward at Long Island College Hospital in Brooklyn. The interviewer noted that the woman appeared upset, at first, when she learned that her new baby would be tested and that if she (the mother) had the virus, the test would show it. "They have no right at all, and I'll sue them if they try it," Alma Velez

Declining Numbers of HIV-Positive Newborns

In the 1990s, the number of infants born in New York who test positive for HIV has declined. Of these newborns, one in four will actually become infected with the virus.

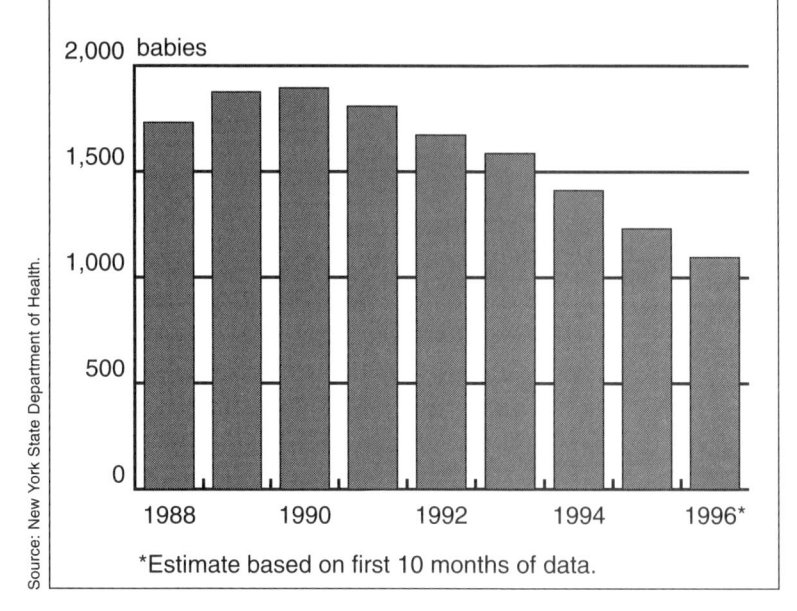

2,000 babies

1988	1990	1992	1994	1996*

*Estimate based on first 10 months of data.

Source: New York State Department of Health.

told a reporter. She then added, "I've always been too scared to do the test, but I always wondered."[54]

The response from doctors also varies. Some question the need to mandate disclosure. Before the New York law took effect, for example, the state's hospitals were required to ask women whether they wanted to know the test results. According to health department figures, about 93 percent agreed to notification. Given this response, one Bronx Lebanon Hospital Center administrator says she prefers voluntary programs over mandatory ones. "I want voluntary programs that strongly encourage women, because in them there are very high acceptance rates for testing. Then women can decide when they are ready to deal with their fears and come forward," says Laurie Solomon, director of the hospital's ambulatory obstetrics and gynecology department.[55]

Many medical experts support prenatal testing for HIV because it offers the hope of preventing the transmission of AIDS to children.

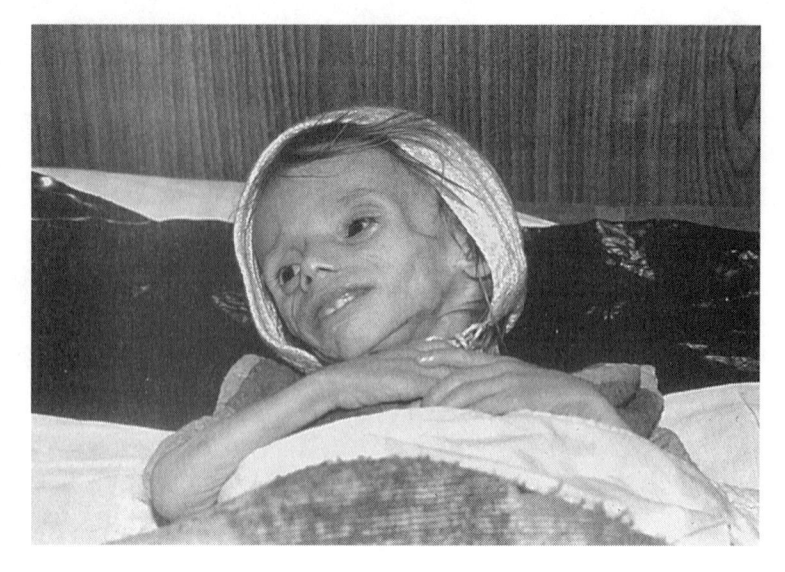

One of the biggest complaints about newborn testing is that it represents too little too late. If the aim of newborn testing is to help the baby, rather than identify the HIV status of the mother, then testing needs to be done before the baby's birth. Dr. Margaret Polaneczky, director of maternal-pediatric HIV counseling and testing at New York Hospital–Cornell Medical Center, says that infant testing and notification laws are misguided:

> All of us in the medical profession would like to see women tested but think it should be done in the prenatal setting. If you're going to mandate that all women be tested without their permission, then at least do it when you can make a difference. Postpartum [after childbirth] is too late.[56]

The most important factor in deciding when to test is the possibility for treatment. Given prenatally and during delivery, the drug AZT can dramatically reduce the likelihood of transmission of the virus from mother to baby. But there are other reasons to test mothers before their babies are born. First, test results may not be available for six weeks after a newborn has been tested: by that time, an HIV-positive mother who breast-feeds her baby has already increased the likelihood of transmission. Additionally, hospitals sometimes have great difficulty finding mothers once they leave the hospital with their babies. At mothers once they leave the hospital with their babies. At the Einstein-Weiler Hospital in the Bronx, for example, the director of newborn services estimates that one-third of HIV-positive mothers are never located. Those who are found have to be persuaded to return to the hospital for the results. "After they've spent three weeks with their babies at home, they don't want to hear that there's a problem," says Dr. Carlos Vega-Rich. "And we have to be vague. We can't mention HIV over the phone, because you need to give the news in a confidential setting."[57]

Differing views about mandatory prenatal testing

For these reasons, many people now say that HIV testing and notification should be required for all pregnant women. In 1996 the American Medical Association—which represents about half the nation's doctors—recommended that all pregnant women be required to undergo testing for the AIDS virus. The AMA also endorsed mandatory testing of newborns. (In contrast, the CDC recommends that all pregnant women be offered a test for HIV but not forced to take one.) Those who favor mandatory prenatal testing say it offers the best hope for preventing the transmission of HIV from mother to child. "The best solution to the problem—indeed, the only truly effective policy—is to test pregnant women directly and routinely, tell them the results and teach them how to behave in the future. If this were done, babies' chances would improve dramatically," writes Barbara J. Ledeen, executive director of the Independent Women's Forum in Washington, D.C.[58]

Pregnant women undergo a variety of tests as part of standard prenatal care. For example, most states have laws or regulations that require women to be tested for syphilis at least once during pregnancy. Newborn infants also undergo routine testing for various conditions including syphilis and hepatitis. Proponents of mandatory prenatal (and newborn) testing say it would be easy enough to add an HIV test to these normal testing regimens. "I'd like to see HIV testing as routine as syphilis testing or eye drops problem," says Dr. Elaine Abrams, director of Pediatric AIDS Care at Harlem Hospital in New York.[59]

The AMA's position does not represent the views of all doctors or even all of its own members. Other doctors' groups, including the AMA's Council on Scientific Affairs, the American College of Obstetricians and Gynecologists, and the American Academy of Pediatrics, have stated their support for voluntary testing. The primary reasons usually involve concern about invading a patient's privacy, overriding a patient's right to determine her own course of medical treatment (particularly in light of the stigma that attaches to a positive HIV test), and the risk of discouraging high-risk pregnant women from obtaining prenatal care. Victoria Thomas of the Pediatric AIDS Foundation in Santa Monica, California, expresses this view:

> It's always been our position that mandatory testing of women or of newborns will drive women from the health-care system, that the sort of punitive nature of mandatory testing is counterproductive, particularly because the women who are at the greatest risk . . . are kind of at the perimeter of the health-care system anyway.[60]

A mother and daughter, both HIV-positive, embrace. The argument against mandatory testing of pregnant women is that it will push away those who are most at risk.

It is for these reasons that many people fear mandatory testing for pregnant women and for other segments of the population.

Finding a balance will not be easy

Many of America's most important laws and traditions have come from Anglo-Saxon legal thinking, which places the utmost value on individual privacy—particularly in matters such as sexual behavior. For many people, mandatory testing signifies a violation of some of the values this nation holds dear. And yet, many others believe that the public health community must use all the tools available to halt the spread of a deadly disease for which there is no cure and no vaccine. Finding a balance between these two positions will not be easy, for American society has shown over and over that it values individual rights as well as the overall public good. Authors William H. Masters, Virginia E. Johnson, and Robert C. Kolodny describe the difficulty of striking such a balance:

> While we fervently hope that mindless panic over the AIDS epidemic will not dictate government policies, we are also convinced that if implementation of effective prevention strategies is delayed by a mistaken belief that this epidemic is now under control or by a single-minded preoccupation with individual autonomy, many millions of lives will be needlessly lost. There is precious little personal freedom in death.[61]

4
The Global Epidemic

EDUCATION AND PREVENTION efforts and dramatic advances in drug treatments have slowed the rate of HIV infection in the United States, Europe, and Australia. But the AIDS virus is spreading quickly elsewhere in the world, especially in sub-Saharan Africa, India, and Thailand. Many researchers say the global epidemic, or pandemic, promises to grow even worse over the next decade. "Projections for the HIV/AIDS pandemic are grim. . . . [I]t is clear that the years to come will be much more difficult than the . . . years since AIDS was first recognized," a team of researchers from the Harvard School of Public Health writes.[62]

A grim future

Projections for the near future are indeed grim. Researchers estimate the number of HIV-infected people worldwide will reach anywhere from 40 to 110 million by the year 2000, with as many as 15 to 50 million in India alone. This represents a substantial increase over a very short period of time. An estimated 26 million people worldwide were infected with the AIDS virus as of January 1995, according to the Global AIDS Policy Coalition, an independent, international organization based at the Harvard School of Public Health. The vast majority of those infections—over 90 percent—have occurred in the developing world. Only about 5 percent have been recorded in North America.

Sub-Saharan Africa is among the worst-afflicted regions in the world. The adult HIV infection rate is higher there

The Worldwide Spread of AIDS

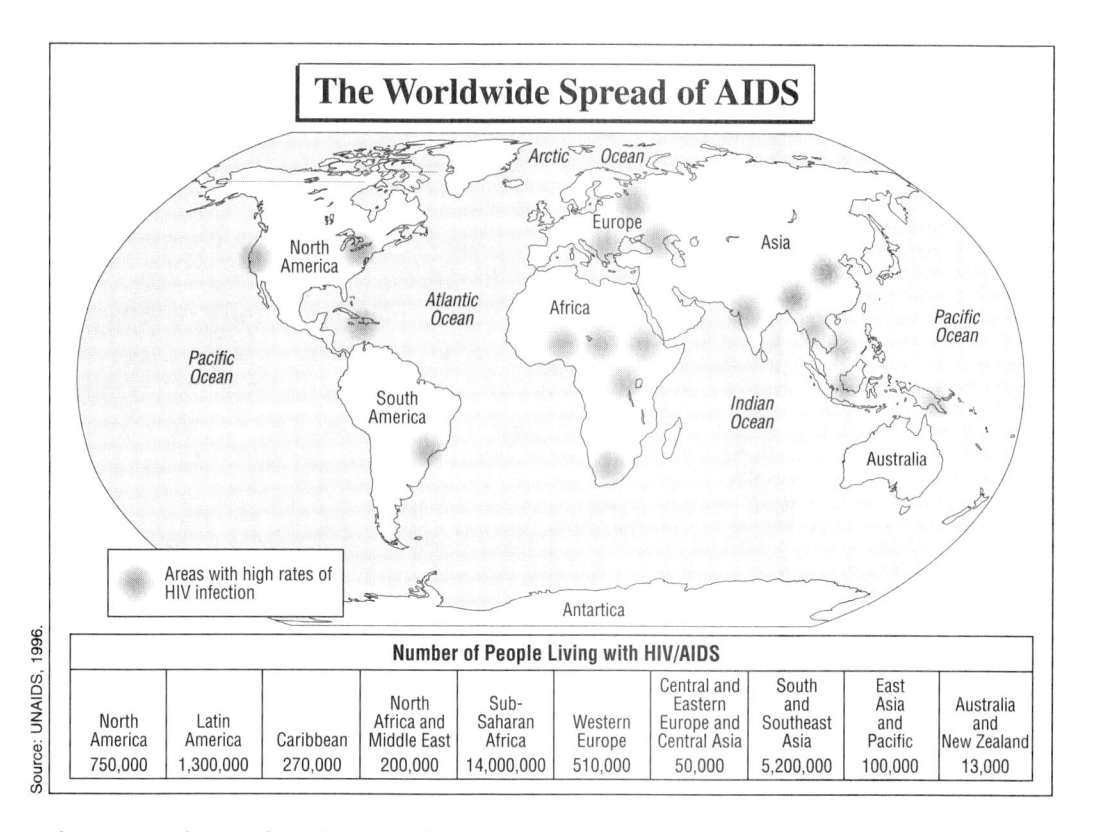

Number of People Living with HIV/AIDS

North America	Latin America	Caribbean	North Africa and Middle East	Sub-Saharan Africa	Western Europe	Central and Eastern Europe and Central Asia	South and Southeast Asia	East Asia and Pacific	Australia and New Zealand
750,000	1,300,000	270,000	200,000	14,000,000	510,000	50,000	5,200,000	100,000	13,000

Source: UNAIDS, 1996.

than anywhere else. Researchers say 17.3 million adult residents of sub-Saharan Africa are infected with the AIDS virus. The region is home to only 10 percent of the world's population, but it accounts for two out of every three HIV-positive adults worldwide. On a global scale, over 80 percent of HIV infections among women and 90 percent of HIV infection among infants are found in sub-Saharan Africa. "By the year 2000, nearly 2 million children in Kenya, Rwanda, Uganda and Zambia will have lost their parents to the disease," *Time* magazine reports.[63]

Researchers have also noted the rapid spread of HIV and AIDS to regions that seemed untouched early in the epidemic. Before the late 1980s, for example, few cases of HIV infection existed in India, Thailand, and Burma. These countries are now experiencing major epidemics. Thailand offers one example of the sudden explosion of HIV infections. That Asian nation has experienced a tenfold increase in HIV infections since early 1990. "In 1987,

Thailand was virtually HIV-free. But now an AIDS epidemic is raging in the country," *Science* magazine reports.[64] Estimates place the number of HIV-infected Thais at around 1 million, a substantial number in a country of 60 million people.

India is another country that has experienced a sudden and rapid rise in the HIV infection rate. Infections there have tripled since 1992. As of January 1997, 3.5 million of India's 950 million people had contracted the AIDS virus. This represents the largest number of HIV cases found in any Asian nation.

High infection rates among women and children

Whereas in many developed nations AIDS first surfaced among primarily homosexual populations, AIDS in much of the developing world has spread mostly through heterosexual contact. About 10 percent of HIV cases in the United States and Western Europe result from heterosexual intercourse. Heterosexual intercourse accounts for more than 90 percent of HIV transmission in Asia and Africa. As a result, the HIV infection rate among women is steadily rising. In the Caribbean, for example, heterosexual transmission is common and the HIV infection rate is nearly even for women and men. Heterosexual intercourse is also the primary means of HIV's spread in sub-Saharan Africa, the only region in the world where more women than men are infected with HIV. Researchers say that eleven to twelve women are infected with HIV for every ten men in sub-Saharan Africa.

High rates of infection among women translate to high rates of infection among children. Most of those infections occur at birth. Research has shown a one-in-four chance that HIV will be passed from an infected mother to her baby. Re-

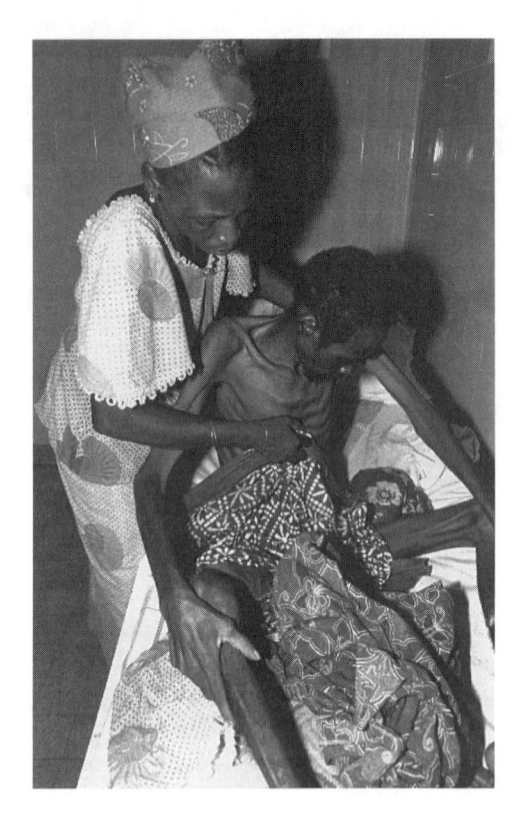

A woman cares for her AIDS-stricken husband in Ivory Coast, Africa. Sub-Saharan Africa is one of the worst-afflicted regions in the world.

search also shows that breast-feeding increases the likelihood of transmission. The World Health Organization (WHO) estimates that nearly a million children are infected with HIV in sub-Saharan Africa alone. Although some of the newest drugs can lessen the chances of transmission from an infected woman to her child, few people in the developing world can afford the necessary course of treatment.

Money matters

Many reasons have been given for the rapid spread of HIV in the developing nations at a time when the HIV infection rate in the United States and other developed nations is slowing. Factors mentioned most often include education, prevention efforts, leadership, cultural and religious values, and money. Some researchers say that discrimination and denial of basic human rights also play a role in the spread of HIV.

As in most things in life, money matters. Poor nations have less money to spend on AIDS prevention and education programs than wealthy nations. In some cases, money may be available but leaders are unconvinced that it should be spent on AIDS programs when their citizens have so many other pressing needs. In the poorest Asian nations, money and expertise are simply not available for AIDS

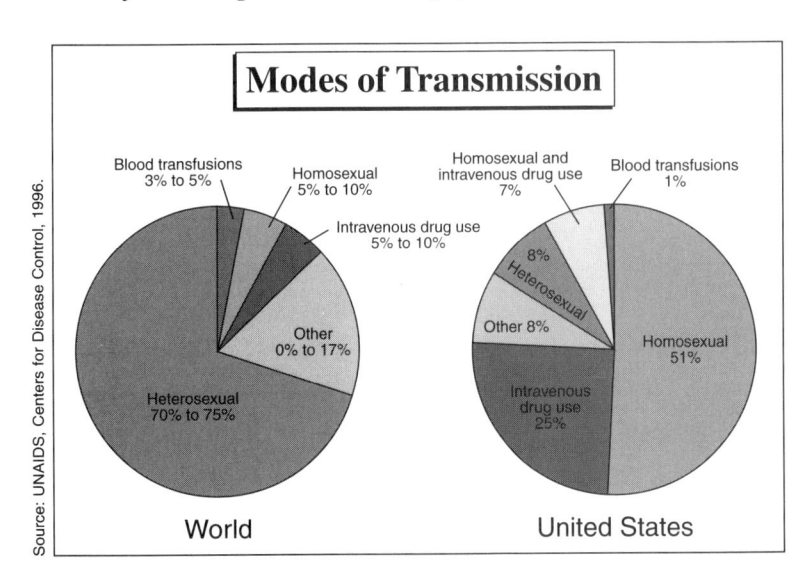

Modes of Transmission

World
- Blood transfusions 3% to 5%
- Homosexual 5% to 10%
- Intravenous drug use 5% to 10%
- Other 0% to 17%
- Heterosexual 70% to 75%

United States
- Homosexual and intravenous drug use 7%
- Blood transfusions 1%
- Heterosexual 8%
- Other 8%
- Homosexual 51%
- Intravenous drug use 25%

Source: UNAIDS, Centers for Disease Control, 1996.

prevention programs. In Cambodia, a nation ravaged by a generation of civil war, many doctors and nurses are still unaware of the most basic facts about HIV and AIDS. According to the *New York Times*, "A recent poll showed that most hospital nurses believed that AIDS was a disease of foreigners, and that it could not be passed between Cambodians. Only 5 percent knew that the virus could be transmitted through a shared needle between drug addicts."[65]

Lack of money also hampers the practice of standard public health measures. AIDS testing is rarely done in the developing countries, for example. Yet the AIDS antibody test, available in the United States since 1985, has dramatically decreased the risk of contracting AIDS through blood transfusions in this country. Moreover, it allows individuals to find out their own HIV status (a precondition for treatment and an essential step in prevention).

Money also plays an important part in treatment options. Few people in the developing world can begin to afford the expensive drug treatments that have been credited with slowing HIV and AIDS in wealthier nations such as the United States. The cost of the new combination drug therapies can run up to $20,000 a year, a sum well beyond the reach of most people in the developing world. Rosemary Omuga, a resident of Nairobi, Kenya, is fairly typical. She tested positive for HIV in 1992 and has since lost her job and her home. "Today she barely earns enough to keep her children alive and cover her $12 monthly rent on a tin-roof shack in one of Nairobi's most fetid slums," *Time* magazine reports.[66] Omuga has no illusions about her chances of obtaining the latest drugs. "We are dying because we don't have medicines. I heard that there are new treatments. But I cannot afford them."[67]

Opposition and lack of commitment

Many fault the world community for not coming to the aid of countries with the greatest financial need. The World Health Organization says it would cost between $1.5 and $2.9 billion per year to establish prevention programs in the developing countries. "Unfortunately, while the global epidemic has intensified and expanded, the global response has stagnated or even declined," the Harvard researchers write.[68]

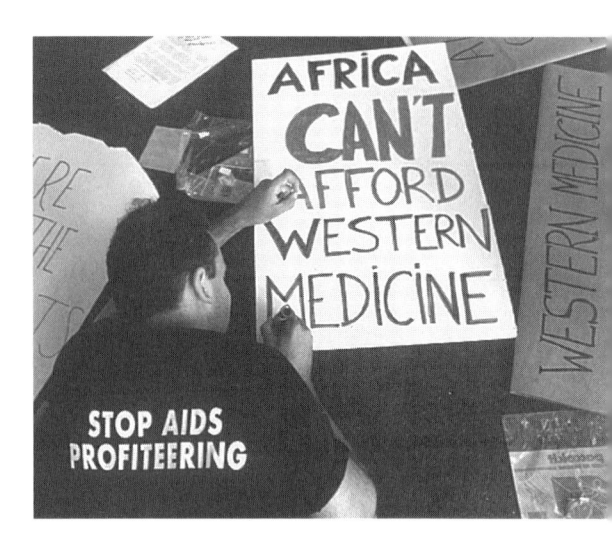

Cultural and religious values have also been cited as an explanation for HIV's spread in some countries. Powerful religious leaders who oppose sex education in any form have blocked some efforts to organize AIDS prevention and education programs. This has occurred in the Philippines, where a prominent Catholic leader has criticized the government's AIDS education and prevention program as "evil." Church leaders have staged protests at which they set boxes of condoms on fire. In Indonesia and Malaysia, Muslim religious fundamentalists accuse AIDS education campaigns of encouraging promiscuity. Indonesia's chief Muslim authority has even demanded that condoms be sold only to married couples, a measure that would leave much of the nation's population unprotected against HIV and AIDS. Women who have AIDS have also fallen victim to cultural beliefs that place them below men in terms of overall value to the society. "For example, women in some countries die of AIDS before they are even diagnosed. They simply aren't considered important enough to qualify for medical attention," one author writes.[69]

The developing nations of Africa, along with developing nations in other parts of the world, lack the money to pay for new drugs available in most Western countries.

The combination of poverty, official opposition or indifference, cultural and religious biases, and fear has resulted in confusion about the most basic facts of HIV and AIDS. "Most of those dying from the disease in rural parts of Africa have no clear idea of what is killing them, let alone how to prevent it," *Time* magazine reports.[70]

Other explanations

Recent research shows a higher risk of HIV infection in populations that have been denied basic human rights. Those who live in the most marginal conditions—without adequate housing, food, education, and health care—are more likely to engage in risky behavior and thus to contract HIV than are those who have their most basic needs met. "The failure to respect human rights can now be identified as a major cause, or even root cause, of societal vulnerability to HIV/AIDS," the Harvard researchers write. "It is now clear that HIV/AIDS is as much about society as it is about a virus."[71]

At least one other factor has been cited in discussions about the rapid spread of HIV in the developing world. Civil wars, some lasting for years, have led to huge shifts in population. In some cases, thousands of people from a single region have abandoned their homes and settled temporarily or permanently in other countries or in other regions of their own countries. Refugees fleeing violence and civil and political strife may actually be hastening the spread of HIV and hampering efforts to assess and control it. A UNAIDS report describes this trend as "particularly troubling" in the Great Lakes region in Africa. It specifically mentions Rwanda and Burundi, which have experienced large population shifts as a result of war and violence and are known in Africa as having the most severe and longest-running HIV epidemics.

The global approach

Despite the complexity of these problems and the difficulty of overcoming them, efforts have been made—both on an international scale and by individual countries. In January 1996, six major UN agencies involved with HIV and AIDS joined together in an effort to confront the prevention and care needs of countries around the world. The participating agencies are the World Health Organization; the UN Children's Fund; the UN Development Programme; the UN Educational, Scientific, and Cultural Organization; the UN Fund for Population; and the World Bank.

A decade earlier, the World Health Organization took on the international AIDS problem with its Global AIDS Strategy, as it was called. As part of this approach, WHO urged countries to develop their own AIDS programs, adapting standard prevention practices to fit individual needs. The organization also offered technical support and help with human and financial resources.

Between 1986 and 1990, WHO's effort resulted in a global AIDS strategy, development of national AIDS programs in most countries, and expansion of community-based efforts. At the same time, the amount of money committed to battling the AIDS pandemic in the developing world rose drastically, from less than $1 million in 1986 to more than $200 million in 1990. "The Global AIDS Strategy's approach proved to be as successful, or more so, than any other public health program seeking to change individual behavior," the Harvard researchers write.[72] But it was not enough to halt the spread of HIV and AIDS.

Efforts by individual countries

Individual countries have also tried to influence the course of HIV's progression. In Uganda, where 15 percent of the adult population is infected with HIV, an AIDS prevention campaign began in the mid-1980s. The campaign included billboards and government warnings. Surveys show that these efforts have brought results. For example, HIV infections among young women fell 35 percent between 1990–1993 and 1994–1995.

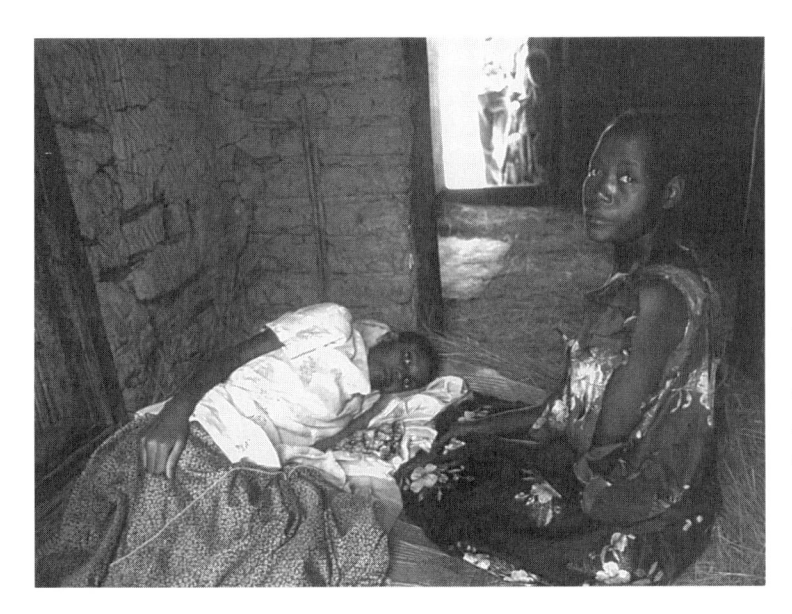

A 1986 photo depicts the devastating toll of AIDS on Uganda's people. An AIDS prevention campaign has shown promising signs of reducing the infection rate in that country.

Thailand also is attempting to slow the spread of HIV and AIDS. An intensive education and public health campaign has had some effect, but infection rates are still high. So Thai leaders have gone even further in their efforts to combat the disease. In recent years, Thailand has established itself as a key testing ground for AIDS vaccines. Thai leaders, and AIDS experts worldwide, believe that a vaccine is the only realistic solution to the AIDS pandemic. Most people believe that a vaccine will one day be developed, but no one can say now when that might be. Researchers have so far been stymied in their efforts to develop a safe and effective vaccine. A surging HIV infection rate bodes poorly for the Thai people. "Faced with this bleak outlook, Thailand is aggressively looking for ways to thwart HIV. Nowhere is this more pronounced than in the country's emerging role as the most important place in the world for testing AIDS vaccines," writes *Science* reporter Jon Cohen.[73]

Antibiotics offer an alternative

Sub-Saharan Africa is also a testing ground, but not for AIDS vaccines. At least two countries are participating in a unique, and so far successful, experiment using antibiotics to slow the spread of AIDS. Antibiotics, which are used to treat sexually transmitted diseases such as syphilis and gonorrhea, can't cure AIDS. Researchers have found, however, that people who have contracted bacterial sex-related diseases are more likely to become exposed to HIV and transmit it. "So if doctors can cure more cases of syphilis, gonorrhea and similar illnesses, they are likely to reduce the number of people who will eventually develop AIDS," *Wall Street Journal* reporter Amanda Bennett writes.[74]

Experts consider this approach one of the first real advances in controlling the spread of AIDS in Africa. Their enthu-

Efforts to slow the spread of AIDS in developing nations include public education. This billboard is part of a public education campaign in Zambia.

siasm stems from two primary factors. One is results: after researchers supplied clinics along Lake Victoria in Tanzania with enough antibiotics and trained workers to treat anyone with symptoms of sexually transmitted disease, HIV infection rates dropped 40 percent. The other factor is cost: in the high-dollar world of HIV and AIDS drugs, antibiotics are a relative bargain. With financial help from the U.S. Agency for International Development (USAID) and a loan from the World Bank, Tanzanian officials are hoping to obtain enough antibiotics and train enough health workers to reach people nationwide. "It's probably the most attainable, effective way to diminish HIV transmission" in the developing countries, says John Cutler, an epidemiologist for USAID in Uganda.[75]

Uganda is also using antibiotics to slow HIV's spread. In another experimental project, researchers are giving antibiotics to every adult living in a district of twenty-six rural communities—regardless of whether they have symptoms of sexually transmitted disease. That project is sponsored by the Ugandan government and by two major U.S. universities, Johns Hopkins and Columbia. Some think that mass treatment may be more effective than treatment of symptoms because sexually transmitted diseases are very common in sub-Saharan Africa.

Reality check

In either case, antibiotics do not represent a miracle solution to the rapid spread of HIV. Although initial results have been encouraging, no one knows for certain whether the same results can be obtained on a broader scale. And although antibiotics cost less than the new drugs being used in the United States and other developed nations, even these drugs are very expensive for the poor nations and poor people of the developing world. In addition, researchers worry that some bacteria responsible for sexually transmitted diseases have already developed resistance to many ordinary antibiotics. Flooding a region or an entire country with more of these drugs could worsen that problem and other problems, as well as defeat the goal of stopping HIV.

Antibiotics offer some hope for controlling AIDS in poor nations that suffer high rates of sexually transmitted diseases.

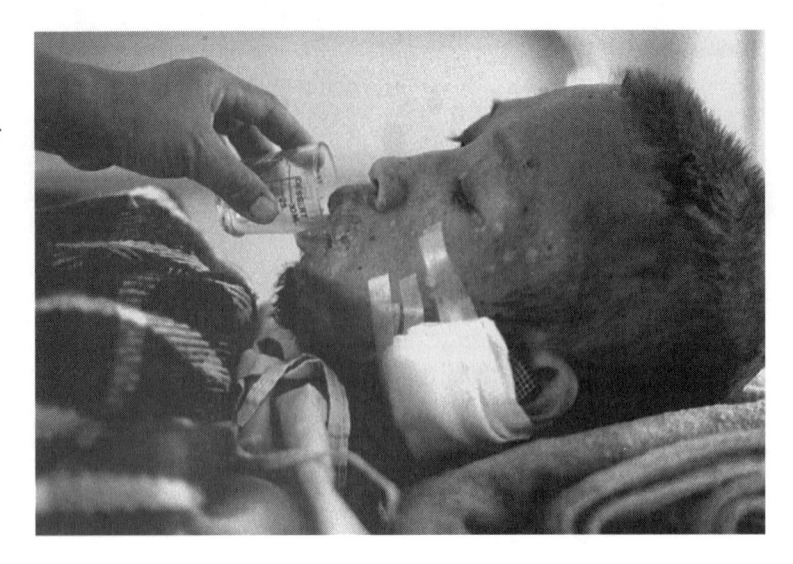

Phillipe Mayaud, manager of the Tanzania project, believes the antibiotic treatment approach is worth pursuing even if, on a wider scale, it does not demonstrate the same level of success achieved in the relatively small experiment. Mayaud says: "It won't have 40% effectiveness in real life. But in a desert, a bucket of water is something."[76]

A warning for the future

The nations of the world face an overwhelming challenge in their efforts to rid the human population of the scourge that is AIDS. Success in this endeavor will take creativity, determination, and possibly more resources than many are presently willing to commit. Despite the difficulties, this effort is essential, both for present and future generations. As Harvard researchers Jonathan M. Mann and Daniel J. M. Tarantola write: "Even as new insights, strategies, and programs are developed against HIV/AIDS, the experience of this pandemic serves as a warning for the future. For today's world is more vulnerable than ever before to the global spread of new and emerging diseases."[77]

5

Is the End in Sight?

WITH ALL THAT is now known about the deadly AIDS virus, scientists still lack the ability to cure the disease or prevent it through a vaccine. Efforts to accomplish both have been under way for many years. Those efforts have been hobbled by the complex and changeable nature of the human immunodeficiency virus (HIV) and by financial limitations and moral and ethical concerns.

Most experts think that a vaccine will one day eliminate AIDS just as other vaccines have done away with the deadly diseases of the recent past—smallpox, polio, and measles, to name a few. With that day still years away, the biggest hope for the present is finding a way to control or manage the disease much as people with diabetes or asthma manage their chronic conditions. Progress on this front has been substantial; evidence of recent successes can be seen in new government statistics that reveal a marked decline in AIDS-related deaths. Nineteen percent fewer AIDS-related deaths occurred between January and September 1996 than during the same period in 1995, according to a 1997 report from the Centers for Disease Control and Prevention. The CDC estimated that 30,700 people died of AIDS in the first nine months of 1996, compared with 37,900 recorded AIDS deaths during the same months in 1995.

While several factors may be responsible for the decline, experts give much of the credit to new drug treatments that keep HIV-infected people alive longer—in some cases years longer—than could be accomplished in the past.

Since a vaccine or cure for AIDS may still be years away, the immediate hope for patients lies in managing the disease.

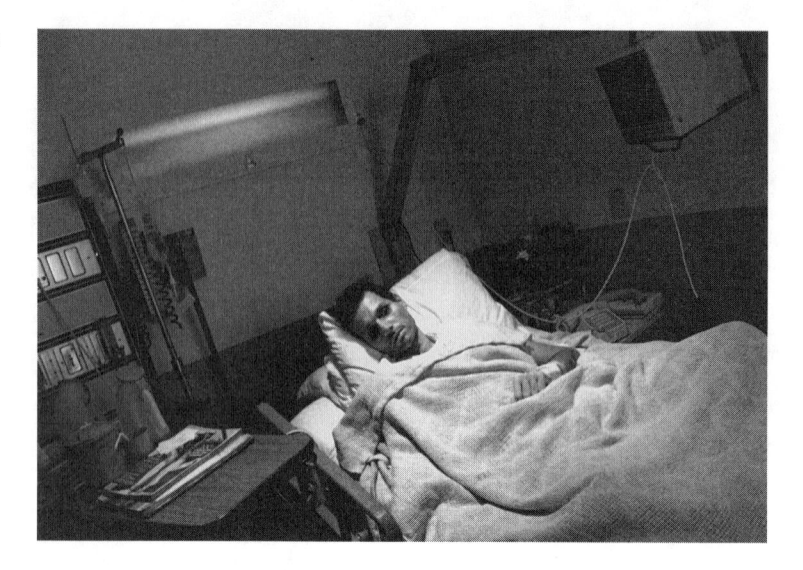

These treatments have shown remarkable results. "For dozens of test subjects—and perhaps thousands of patients now in treatment—the prospect of imminent death is giving way to a remarkable rebound in health," writes *Wall Street Journal* reporter Michael Waldholz. "It is the first time any medical therapy has shown the potential for rescuing people on the verge of succumbing to the disease."[78]

Despite this new, hopeful turn of events, few experts are willing to claim victory in the fight against AIDS. Past declarations of success have too often ended abruptly in disappointment. Jon Cohen of *Science* magazine writes: "AIDS research ricochets from breathtaking optimism to stomach-wrenching disappointment so frequently that many people have become numb to new results."[79]

Nevertheless, some express hope that the end of AIDS may be in sight, a view reflected by *Time* magazine reporter Christine Gorman: "After 15 years of horror, denial and disappointment, the pendulum may at long last be swinging against AIDS."[80]

A sign of hope

A first sign of hope came in 1986 when a National Cancer Institute study revealed that the drug AZT could slow the progression of AIDS. AZT, also known as zidovudine or by the brand name Retrovir, was developed in 1964 to fight cancer. It was ineffective against cancer but showed promise years later against retroviruses, the family of viruses to which HIV belongs. When National Cancer Institute researchers tested AZT's potential as an AIDS fighter, they achieved dramatic results. By the fourth week, AZT-treated patients had regained weight while patients who received a placebo lost weight. At the end of six months only one person in the AZT group was dead, while 19 of the 137 patients in the other group had died. The evidence of success seemed so overwhelming that researchers took the unusual step of halting the study in order to seek federal approval for immediate distribution of the drug to AIDS patients. In 1987 the U.S. Food and Drug Administration approved the experimental use of AZT, the first drug shown to fight AIDS.

Hopes soared as word of AZT's successes spread. By blocking reverse transcriptase, an enzyme needed in the early stage of HIV reproduction, AZT could actually extend the lives of people with AIDS. Researchers have identified other benefits of AZT, as well: it decreases the occurrence of opportunistic infections; it helps to protect the brain against damage from the AIDS virus; and it reduces by two-thirds the risk of HIV transmission from a pregnant woman to her baby.

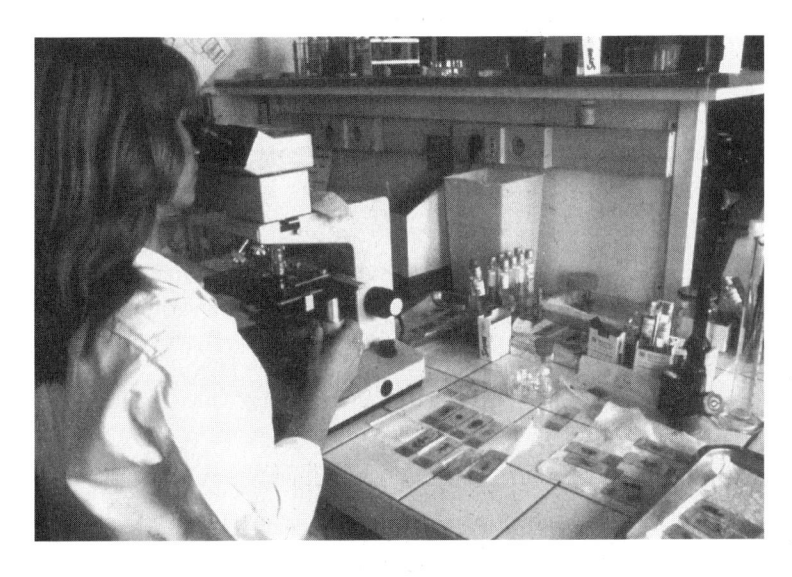

A scientist studies AZT, the drug hailed in the 1980s as capable of slowing HIV and improving the health of patients.

By 1990, AZT had become the top AIDS treatment drug. "But the more time passes, the greater the disappointment becomes," writes physician and author Mirko D. Grmek.[81] AZT is not the cure researchers and AIDS activists had hoped for. Although it can extend the lives of people who have been diagnosed with AIDS, it has had little effect on HIV-infected people who have not yet developed the disease. Experience has also shown that patients who use AZT eventually suffer side effects that add to the damage caused by HIV.

Problems with AZT

The trouble with AZT is that it is highly toxic, not only to HIV-infected cells but also to healthy cells. When doctors first began prescribing AZT as a treatment for AIDS they recommended high doses at frequent intervals. Medical researchers have since learned that the drug is more effective when given in smaller doses and less frequently, but undesirable side effects persist. Between 40 and 80 percent of all AIDS patients who have taken AZT have had to discontinue treatment because of side effects, which include anemia, nausea, diarrhea, and damage to the liver, bone marrow, and nerves.

A further drawback is that most people taking AZT soon develop resistance to it. To get around this problem, AIDS researchers have turned to a multiple-drug approach. The idea of using several drugs at once is well established in another area of medicine—cancer treatment. Cancer specialists, also called oncologists, have long used drug combinations to kill cancerous cells. *Time* magazine's Gorman writes:

> Oncologists have learned that it is often better to combine the firepower of several different . . . drugs than to rely on any single medication to destroy cancer cells. Too often, they have found, the one-drug approach allows a few malignant cells to survive and blossom into an even more lethal tumor.[82]

A similar problem exists with HIV. When doctors prescribe a single drug—AZT, for example—any viral particles the drug fails to kill give rise to a mutation, a new strain of HIV that resists later doses of the drug and renders it useless. But if doctors prescribe three drugs at once, the AIDS virus has to come up with three mutations all at the same time to thwart the attack. This is difficult even for the wily AIDS virus.

New research strongly supports the combined-drug approach for fighting AIDS. "Several studies reported in 1996 found that a combination of drugs could sharply curtail the amount of virus in the bloodstream—in many cases reducing it to undetectable levels," reporter Sarah Richardson writes in *Discover* magazine.[83] AZT is one of the antiviral drugs used in these combination treatments, commonly known as "drug cocktails." Other frequently prescribed antiviral drugs, like AZT, are known by their abbreviations: ddI, ddC, D4T, and 3TC.

An AIDS patient shows off the array of pills he takes daily. Patients must stick to a strict schedule for taking medication for the treatment to be successful.

A rising star

But the real star of today's HIV/AIDS treatment arsenal, and the key ingredient in most drug cocktails, is a new class of antiviral drugs called protease inhibitors. In the fight against AIDS, protease inhibitors keep infected cells from producing new virus by blocking the enzymatic substance called protease, which is crucial in later stages of the HIV life cycle.

Scientists first identified the HIV protease in 1986. Once they understood its role in the reproduction of the virus, they set out to find a drug that would block this activity. The first protease inhibitors proved too toxic in both animals and humans. By 1994, however, some of the new drugs were producing good results. "Where AZT merely slowed viral reproduction, the protease inhibitors shut it down almost completely," *Time* magazine's Gorman writes.[84]

The development of protease inhibitors also provided a few scientists with the tool they needed to test another theory about the behavior of HIV. According to this new theory, HIV began to reproduce in the host immediately after infection and remained active in the body forever after. This theory conflicted with the widely held view that HIV was inactive in the body for three to ten years after infection until some unknown event awakened the virus and caused it to reproduce. "In this [early] picture, the AIDS virus spent most of its life hibernating before starting its final, deadly assault," writes Gorman.[85] Based on this view of HIV's behavior, doctors usually delayed treatment until later stages when the infection had become very obvious.

Pioneering AIDS researcher David Ho and his colleagues determined that HIV multiplies in the body within weeks of infection. This groundbreaking discovery led doctors to begin treating the virus in its early stages.

A theory overturned

Among the scientists who questioned the accepted view of HIV was David Ho, director of the Aaron Diamond AIDS Research Center in New York City since 1990. Ho had been searching for a way to test his theory, and the new protease inhibitors gave him that opportunity. Research conducted by Ho and others between 1995 and 1997 overturned the hibernation theory and brought about a major change in the world's understanding of the AIDS virus. This work also led to an important shift in treatment strategy.

Research by Ho and other scientists showed that the virus silently multiplies over and over within the first few weeks of infection. This replication had gone largely unnoticed because it occurs in the lymph nodes (and possibly elsewhere), safely out of sight of traditional tests that measure the amount of virus in the blood. "The results [of tests by Ho and his colleagues] showed that in every day of every year, in every infected person, HIV produced not thousands, not millions, but *billions* of copies of itself," Gorman writes.[86]

For the first time, researchers realized that withholding treatment until later stages of illness might lessen the odds of recovery. By the time the virus shows up in measurable levels in the bloodstream, it has usually destroyed the lymph nodes, along with any real chance of saving the immune system. This means that the best time for treatment is probably found in the early stages of infection rather than in later stages of the disease. Most doctors have changed their treatment strategies to reflect this new view of HIV.

Drug cocktails bring results

The combination of new drugs and early and aggressive treatment seems to be working. In 1996 Ho reported results from one drug trial involving nine men who received three drugs—a protease inhibitor, AZT, and 3TC—within ninety days of being infected with HIV. "Within a few months of treatment," *Discover* magazine reports, "HIV could not be detected in the men's blood. Even after a year of treatment no trace of it could be found."[87] Other studies' trials have had similar successes.

Although hope of long-term recovery probably is unrealistic in people in the later phases of AIDS, study results have been encouraging even for some of those patients. In one 1996 study conducted at four medical centers around the country, New York University's Roy Gulick and other researchers gave three drugs to ninety-seven patients who had taken AZT for more than two years. "After another year of treatment with AZT, now supplemented with 3TC and a protease inhibitor, some 80 percent of the patients showed no trace of the virus at all," writes Sarah Richardson in *Discover*.[88] Researchers conducting another study, involving 1,090 patients with advanced AIDS, reported in 1996 that subjects who added a protease inhibitor to their drug treatment had a 50 percent lower mortality rate than those receiving a placebo.

Drug cocktails containing protease inhibitors—especially if given soon after infection—may be the key to eventually ridding a patient's body of the AIDS virus. For now, however, they offer the smaller but still significant advantage of giving the body time to rebuild damaged organs and return to some normal functioning. As Gorman writes:

> Within weeks of starting combination therapy, 7 out of 10 men and women with AIDS begin to get better. . . . Relieved of the burden of fighting HIV, their long-suffering immune systems can finally tackle the deadly fungal and bacterial infections that have taken hold in their lungs, intestines, and brains. Fevers break; lesions disappear; energy returns.[89]

The return of even a measure of stability to the body cannot replace defensive reserves depleted through a decade of fighting HIV, however. Researchers are exploring various options for rebuilding the battered immune systems of AIDS patients. One option is to grow replacement cells in a laboratory and transplant them into a recovering patient. But such treatments are still a long way off.

Limitations

Triple-drug therapy offers the most promising treatment option ever developed for HIV and AIDS, but it falls short of a cure. As with previous treatments, the new drugs have limitations. Under the right circumstances, drug cocktails seem capable of clearing the bloodstream of HIV, but they have difficulty reaching into the brain, the lymph nodes, the spinal fluid, and other parts of the body where HIV hides. Research is under way to determine whether certain drug combinations can rid these organs of the AIDS virus. Early results of at least two studies, one being conducted by a Canadian team and the other by researchers in the Netherlands and Minnesota, have shown success. But researchers caution that they will have to follow patients' progress for two or three years before it will be possible to say whether the virus has been purged from all tissues in the body.

Side effects are another concern. They are milder with triple-drug therapy than with other treatments, but some patients experience diarrhea and fatigue, as well as spasms, kidney stones, and liver damage. Late-stage AIDS patients, who benefit less from treatment than those who begin the drugs in the earliest phases of infection, will probably have to stay on combination therapy for the rest of their lives.

The unknowns

Much is still unknown about HIV, AIDS, and the new drug treatments. For some scientists the unknowns are even more troubling than the documented limitations. For example, researchers do not know whether successful HIV treatment will also prevent transmission from one person to another. And, while combination drug therapy may postpone the progression of AIDS for a few years, or even longer, researchers believe that the immune systems of late-stage patients will collapse despite aggressive treatment. Perhaps most troubling of all, researchers do not know whether HIV will mutate into a strain that resists the new drug combinations, thus repeating the pattern seen with other treatments. As one reporter writes: "This is undeniably an exciting time for AIDS researchers, but these high hopes are tempered by the realization that, so far, HIV in time has developed resistance to every drug—and every drug combination—thrown at it."[90]

On this last point, researchers and others received some disappointing news in September 1997. According to study results presented at an infectious disease conference in Toronto, Canada, the virus appears to be growing resistant to the new protease inhibitors. Data from the University of California's large public AIDS clinic at San Francisco General Hospital show that the drugs are beginning to fail in about half of all those treated. Researchers say other large AIDS clinics have had similar experiences. Their research did not explore the reasons for the apparent failure rate.

However, three other research teams announced somewhat different findings in November 1997. Researchers from Johns Hopkins University, the University of California, San Diego, and the National Institute of Allergy and Infectious Diseases say their studies show that the virus has not developed resistance in people who follow the precise schedule for taking their medications. (Lapses in the strict medication regimen have been suggested as one explanation for the drug failures encountered in other studies.) However, the researchers also found that the new drugs do not eliminate HIV from all parts of the body. Working independently, all three teams found traces of the virus in the immune systems of patients with undetectable levels of HIV in their blood. This means that patients must continue taking the drugs on a strict schedule and possibly for the rest of their lives.

Cost is an obstacle

This leads to another problem that threatens to undermine the early successes of the new drugs: cost. A typical triple-drug treatment regimen consists of fourteen to twenty pills taken every day of every month of every year for several years—and possibly for the rest of the patient's life. A supply that large can cost a great deal of money, especially while the drugs are still relatively new. When antiviral drugs such as AZT first came on the market they, too, were expensive. In 1987 a year's worth of AZT, consisting of the 1,200-milligram daily doses commonly prescribed at that time, cost about $10,000. Price cuts by the manufacturer and decreases in recommended dosages have brought the price down to between $6,400 and $3,000 per year, depending on how far the disease has progressed. Triple-drug therapy with a protease inhibitor costs between $12,000 and $16,000 a year. Many private insurance companies and government-funded medical insurance programs cover some AIDS treatments. But the new protease inhibitors are so expensive that some state programs simply do not offer them to patients. As of August 1996, for example, more than thirty states offered at least one protease drug. Seventeen offered none.

Access to the latest drugs is an even more serious problem in Africa, India, and Thailand. The cost of the new combination therapies puts them far out of reach of all but the wealthiest people in these regions. As one reporter writes:

> For the majority of those with HIV outside the U.S. and Europe, the cost of the new "cocktail" treatments seems a cruel joke. The average Kenyan would exhaust his annual income

Members of ACT UP (AIDS Coalition to Unleash Power) protest the high cost and inaccessibility of AIDS drugs.

in less than a week on the regimen. In India . . . even a two-drug treatment can run to $3,500 a month, or more than 75 times the monthly earnings of poor laborers, who are the prime victims of the disease.[91]

Closer to home, in Mexico, the situation is not much better. The typical AIDS cocktail containing a protease inhibitor can run $1,200 a month, and a one-month supply of AZT ranges from $150 to $448. Few individuals can afford those prices and the government also lacks the money to subsidize them. Patients at the only country's government-run AIDS clinic in the populous city of Tijuana, in Baja California, receive free HIV testing, AIDS counseling, and treatment for infections such as tuberculosis and pneumonia. But the latest drugs are beyond the reach of even the government-run clinic. Referring to the new drug cocktails, the clinic's director says, "Here we don't have a choice because they're not accessible. It is too costly."[92]

Poor nations may be able to treat secondary infections such as tuberculosis, but they rarely have money for expensive new AIDS drugs.

"We must develop vaccines"

Most experts agree that drugs—no matter how much success they have in managing HIV and AIDS—are too expensive to be a solution to the worldwide AIDS epidemic. These experts say that an AIDS vaccine, which can be administered quickly and cheaply to all the world's people, is the only realistic way to do away with AIDS. H. R. Shepherd, who heads an important private research foundation, makes this point:

> The human suffering and economic crisis caused by AIDS point to a single imperative: We must develop vaccines to prevent, and eventually eradicate, HIV. Vaccines are the most cost-effective medical intervention ever devised. They stop epidemics and prevent diseases for a fraction of the treatment costs.[93]

Toward this end, research has been under way for more than a decade. But results have been disappointing. No one has developed a usable vaccine (one that provides immunity without causing serious illness) or even one deemed worthy of large-scale tests on human populations.

Several factors may explain the lack of success in developing a vaccine. Some say the obstacles are financial: too little public money spent on AIDS vaccine development and too little financial return for private companies. Less than 10 percent of the National Institutes of Health AIDS research funding for 1995 went toward development of a vaccine, for example. Others cite ethical and moral obstacles: no one knows how experimental vaccines will affect the health of human test subjects, and this uncertainty has held up some promising research efforts. One project, conducted by scientists at Harvard's New England Regional Primate Center, involves macaque monkeys and an experimental vaccine made from an attenuated, or weakened, form of simian immunodeficiency virus (SIV), which is the monkey version of the AIDS virus. The vaccine appears to have prevented infection in the monkeys that were injected with an exceptionally large dose of SIV. "Virtually everyone agrees that . . . [the] experiment is a landmark in AIDS research," one reporter writes.[94] Since, however, the research community cannot agree on whether human testing of this type of vaccine can be done safely, its potential effects on people with AIDS are unknown.

HIV's complexity poses a major obstacle

Nearly all agree that one of the biggest obstacles to developing an AIDS vaccine is the complexity of the virus that causes the disease. HIV simply does not act like other known viruses. Unlike other viruses, it attacks and eventually destroys the immune system, which is the body's only means of producing disease-fighting antibodies. Antibodies that are produced naturally (or induced by experimental vaccines) before the immune system collapses are often useless because HIV changes form so rapidly and so often that the antibodies fail to recognize the characteristics of the virus they are supposed to neutralize. Further complicating the search for a vaccine is the fact that scientists have identified about a dozen different strains of HIV worldwide, and a vaccine developed against one strain may not provide immunity against any other. One expert sums up the difficulty of AIDS vaccine development this way:

> In most natural viral infections, illness occurs, an immune response develops, and if the illness is not acutely fatal, recovery ensues. In AIDS, most patients develop antibodies and even killer T cells against the virus, yet they fail to clear the virus and inexorably succumb to AIDS. The challenge is how to achieve something that nature has not succeeded in doing.[95]

More than a decade of research has brought scientists closer to meeting that challenge, but much more work lies ahead.

The search for a vaccine

Early research efforts followed traditional approaches to developing vaccines. As researchers learned more about HIV, however, many came to believe that traditional vaccines made from weakened or inactivated forms of the virus posed too much risk. They could not be sure that these vaccines would not cause the illness they were intended to prevent. "There is simply no way to guarantee that the viruses in a vaccine made of inactivated HIV will remain inactive," writes one reporter. "Similarly, any merely weakened strain of HIV might still overpower the human immune system."[96] Other early AIDS vaccines, based on different principles, were safe but ineffective against HIV.

Progress in the long-stalled search seemed close at hand in early 1994 as American researchers prepared for the first large-scale tests of two promising vaccines, both made from genetically engineered material. But the National Institutes of Health called off the tests in June of that year because, as one reporter writes, the vaccines "didn't look promising enough."[97] Although the two vaccines, originally developed by a pair of California firms, Genentech of San Francisco and Chiron Corporation of Emeryville, will not be tested in the United States, other countries are free to try them. AIDS researchers in Thailand, a country that faces a surging AIDS epidemic, plan to move ahead with small-scale tests of the two vaccines. If all goes well, large-scale testing could begin by the year 2000.

Despite the many obstacles and setbacks, research on AIDS vaccines continues. By mid-1997, more than two dozen vaccines had been tested in small-scale human stud-

AIDS activists protest the lack of progress on finding a cure for the disease.

ies. Small-scale studies (also called trials) help scientists determine the safety of an experimental vaccine as well as its ability to stimulate immune responses. Small-scale trials usually precede a large-scale trial, which involves several thousand people and many millions of dollars. One small-scale test, covering about four hundred volunteers, began in the United States in mid-1997. The vaccine being tested is based on a canary-pox virus that contains several genes from the AIDS virus. Test subjects, who are individuals at high risk of HIV infection because of a history of sexual promiscuity or intravenous drug use, will also receive genetically engineered booster shots.

Preliminary safety tests in humans (in this case, healthy, uninfected men) are also being conducted using a genetically engineered vaccine that has had good results in tests on chimpanzees. This vaccine has successfully protected two chimpanzees against HIV. Chimpanzees are often used in such tests because their immune system is

Vaccine research represents the best hope for stopping AIDS worldwide, but for those who already have HIV or AIDS, such as this eight-year-old girl, the future is uncertain.

similar to that of humans. More than a year after each chimp was vaccinated and then given enough AIDS virus to infect 250 animals, tests show their bodies to be completely free of the virus.

Vaccine research gets a political boost

The AIDS vaccine development effort got a political boost in May 1997 from President Bill Clinton. Clinton called for development of an AIDS vaccine within a decade. As part of his call for a vaccine to become "a new national goal for science in the age of biology," Clinton pledged to establish an AIDS vaccine research center at the National Institutes of Health.[98] The NIH research center is to take the lead in the worldwide effort to develop a vaccine. Although the president's announcement did not come with a promise of more money for research, most agree that a higher political profile can't hurt and might even prompt Congress to increase funds for AIDS vaccine projects.

Despite the president's call for an AIDS vaccine within a decade, no one is predicting that such a product will actually exist by that time. Researchers have been stung before by predictions of success where HIV and AIDS are concerned. Even Clinton tried to temper his pledge by adding that "there are no guarantees. It will take energy and focus and demand great effort from our greatest minds."[99]

"We can only hope"

Many diseases have ravaged human populations throughout history. Some, like smallpox, endured over many, many centuries. This sometimes disfiguring and often fatal disease has troubled humanity since the time of the ancient Egyptians. So when scientists finally perfected a vaccine against smallpox in the nineteenth century, it was indeed a triumph. A worldwide immunization campaign ensued, with victory declared in 1980 when the World Health Organization officially announced the eradication of smallpox.

The world now awaits a similar outcome for AIDS. How long it will take, no one can say. Clyde B. McCoy and James A. Inciardi write: "We can only hope that AIDS will not endure for as long as smallpox before it is finally conquered."[100]

Notes

Introduction

1. H. R. Shepherd, "Still Needed: An AIDS Vaccine," *Wall Street Journal*, December 3, 1996, p. A22.

2. Gail B. Stewart, *People with AIDS*. San Diego: Lucent Books, 1996, p. 75.

3. Quoted in Stewart, *People with AIDS*, p. 89.

Chapter 1: Unraveling the Mystery

4. Clyde B. McCoy and James A. Inciardi, *Sex, Drugs, and the Continuing Spread of AIDS*. Los Angeles: Roxbury Publishing, 1995, p. 3.

5. Mirko D. Grmek, *History of AIDS: Emergence and Origin of a Modern Pandemic*. Princeton, NJ: Princeton University Press, 1990, p. 5.

6. Grmek, *History of AIDS*, p. 7.

7. Randy Shilts, *And the Band Played On: Politics, People, and the AIDS Epidemic*. New York: St. Martin's Press, 1987, p. 37.

8. Shilts, *And the Band Played On*, p. 49.

9. Shilts, *And the Band Played On*, p. 49.

10. Shilts, *And the Band Played On*, p. 72.

11. Shilts, *And the Band Played On*, p. 71.

12. McCoy and Inciardi, *Sex, Drugs, and the Continuing Spread of AIDS*, p. 9.

13. Grmek, *History of AIDS*, p. 36.

14. Grmek, *History of AIDS*, p. 38.

15. McCoy and Inciardi, *Sex, Drugs, and the Continuing Spread of AIDS*, p. 9.

16. Grmek, *History of AIDS*, p. 47.

17. Paul Harding Douglas and Laura Pinsky, *The Essential AIDS Fact Book*. New York: Pocket Books, 1996, p. 1.

18. Grmek, *History of AIDS*, p. 90.

Chapter 2: The Challenge of Preventing AIDS

19. Jeff Stryker, Thomas J. Coates, and Pamela DeCarlo et al., "Prevention of HIV Infection: Looking Back, Looking Ahead," *JAMA*, April 12, 1995, p. 1,143.

20. Stryker, Coates, and DeCarlo et al., "Prevention of HIV Infection," p. 1,143.

21. William H. Masters, Virginia E. Johnson, and Robert C. Kolodny, *Crisis: Heterosexual Behavior in the Age of AIDS*. New York: Grove Press, 1988, p. 141.

22. Quoted in Julie Shippen, "AIDS Rates Rising for 30- to 40-Year-Old Heterosexual Women," *Corpus Christi Caller Times* (from Knight-Ridder news service), August 29, 1996, p. C6.

23. Bonnie Shullenberger, "Needle-Exchange Programs Will Not Prevent AIDS," in Michael D. Biskup and Karin L. Swisher, eds., *AIDS*. San Diego: Greenhaven Press, 1992, p. 137.

24. Quoted in McCoy and Inciardi, *Sex, Drugs, and the Continuing Spread of AIDS*, p. 128.

25. Shullenberger, "Needle-Exchange Programs," p. 137.

26. Quoted in Julie Shippen, "AIDS Rates Rising for 30- to 40-Year-Old Heterosexual Women," p. C6.

27. Masters, Johnson, and Kolodny, *Crisis*, p. 141.

28. Ken Sidey, "Abstinence Will Prevent AIDS," in Biskup and Swisher, *AIDS*, p. 150.

29. Sidey, "Abstinence Will Prevent AIDS," p. 150.

30. Herbert Ratner, "Promoting Abstinence Will Stop AIDS," in Charles P. Cozic, ed., *The AIDS Crisis*. San Diego: Greenhaven Press, 1991, p. 232.

31. Andy Humm and Frances Kunreuther, "Educating Teenagers About AIDS Can Help Stop Its Spread," in Biskup and Swisher, eds., *AIDS*, p. 146.

32. Quoted in Linda Marsa, "Education Can Help Young Adults Avoid AIDS," in Cozic, *The AIDS Crisis*, p. 209.

33. Masters, Johnson, and Kolodny, *Crisis*, p. 143.

34. McCoy and Inciardi, *Sex, Drugs, and the Continuing Spread of AIDS*, p. 126.

35. Masters, Johnson, and Kolodny, *Crisis*, p. 143.

Chapter 3: Testing for HIV Infection

36. Shilts, *And the Band Played On*, p. 539.

37. Helen Mathews Smith, "The Deadly Politics of AIDS," *Wall Street Journal*, October 25, 1995, p. A14.

38. Sandor Katz, "AIDS Testing Is Ineffective and Discriminatory," in Cozic, *The AIDS Crisis*, p. 132.

39. Chandler Burr, "The AIDS Exception: Privacy vs. Public Health," *Atlantic Monthly*, June 1997, p. 58.

40. Shilts, *And the Band Played On*, p. 514.

41. Shilts, *And the Band Played On*, p. 540.

42. Quoted in Burr, "The AIDS Exception," p. 58.

43. Burr, "The AIDS Exception," p. 58.

44. Shilts, *And the Band Played On*, p. 540.

45. Burr, "The AIDS Exception," p. 59.

46. Helene D. Gayle, "Letters: The AIDS Exception," *Atlantic Monthly*, September 1997, p. 8.

47. Katz, "AIDS Testing," p. 133.

48. Burr, "The AIDS Exception," p. 66.

49. Tracey Hooker and Dianna Gordon, "Mothers and AIDS," *State Legislatures*, April 1995, pp. 30–33.

50. Hooker and Gordon, "Mothers and AIDS," pp. 30–33.

51. Lisa Merkel-Holguin, "Mandatory Testing of Infants Will Not Control the Spread of AIDS," in Daniel A. Leone, ed., *The Spread of AIDS*. San Diego: Greenhaven Press, 1997, p. 59.

52. Quoted in Nat Hentoff, "Censoring the Right to Live," *Progressive*, February 1995, pp. 19–20.

53. Quoted in Deborah Sontag, "HIV Testing for Newborns Debated Anew," *New York Times*, February 10, 1997, pp. A1+.

54. Quoted in Sontag, "HIV Testing for Newborns," pp. A1+.
55. Quoted in Sontag, "HIV Testing for Newborns," pp. A1+.
56. Quoted in Sontag, "HIV Testing for Newborns," pp. A1+.
57. Quoted in Sontag, "HIV Testing for Newborns," pp. A1+.
58. Barbara J. Ledeen, "Sacrificing Babies on the Altar of Privacy," *Wall Street Journal*, August 3, 1995, p. A8.
59. Quoted in Hentoff, "Censoring the Right to Live," pp. 19–20.
60. Quoted in Laura Beil, "AMA Backs HIV Test for Pregnant Women," *Dallas Morning News*, June 28, 1996, p. A1+.
61. Masters, Johnson, and Kolodny, *Crisis*, p. 177.

Chapter 4: The Global Epidemic

62. Jonathan M. Mann and Daniel J. M. Tarantola, "A Global Strategy Is Needed to Control the Spread of AIDS," in Leone, *The Spread of AIDS*, p. 16.
63. Andrew Purvis, "The Global Epidemic," *Time*, December 30, 1996/January 6, 1997, p. 78.
64. Jon Cohen, "Thailand Weighs AIDS Vaccine Tests," *Science*, November 10, 1995, p. 904.
65. Philip Shenon, "AIDS Epidemic, Late to Arrive, Now Explodes in Populous Asia," *New York Times*, January 21, 1996, p. A8.
66. Purvis, "The Global Epidemic," p. 76.
67. Quoted in Purvis, "The Global Epidemic," p. 76.
68. Mann and Tarantola, "A Global Strategy," p. 14.
69. Tim Unsworth, "Governments Should Combat the Spread of AIDS," in Leone, *The Spread of AIDS*, p. 27.
70. Purvis, "The Global Epidemic," p. 78.
71. Mann and Tarantola, "A Global Strategy," p. 10.
72. Mann and Tarantola, "A Global Strategy," p. 14.
73. Cohen, "Thailand Weighs AIDS Vaccine Tests," p. 904.
74. Amanda Bennett, "A New Regimen: Africa's AIDS

Experts Turn to Antibiotics to Slow the Epidemic," *Wall Street Journal*, December 27, 1996, p. A1+.

75. Quoted in Bennett, "A New Regimen," pp. A1+.
76. Quoted in Bennett, "A New Regimen," pp. A1+.
77. Mann and Tarantola, "A Global Strategy," p. 16.

Chapter 5: Is the End in Sight?

78. Michael Waldholz, "Strong Medicine: New Drug 'Cocktails' Mark Exciting Turn in the War on AIDS," *Wall Street Journal*, June 14, 1996, pp. A1+.

79. Jon Cohen, "Results on New AIDS Drugs Bring Cautious Optimism," *Science*, February 9, 1996, p. 755.

80. Christine Gorman, "The Disease Detective," *Time*, December 30, 1996/January 6, 1997, p. 58.

81. Grmek, *History of AIDS*, p. 185.
82. Gorman, "The Disease Detective," p. 62.
83. Sarah Richardson, "AIDS: Crushing HIV," *Discover*, January 1997, p. 28.
84. Gorman, "The Disease Detective," p. 61.
85. Gorman, "The Disease Detective," p. 59.
86. Gorman, "The Disease Detective," p. 62.
87. Richardson, "Crushing HIV," p. 28.
88. Richardson, "Crushing HIV," p. 28.
89. Gorman, "The Disease Detective," p. 62.
90. Cohen, "Results on New AIDS Drugs," p. 756.
91. Purvis, "The Global Epidemic," p. 78.
92. Quoted in Dana Calvo, "Advances in U.S. AIDS Treatments Bad News for Victims in Mexico," *Corpus Christi Caller Times* (from the Associated Press), March 22, 1997, p. D19.
93. Shepherd, "Still Needed: An AIDS Vaccine," p. A22.
94. Daniel Q. Haney, "AIDS Vaccine May Work—if Researchers Ever Dare Test It on Humans," *Corpus Christi Caller Times* (from the Associated Press), May 25, 1997, p. A23.
95. Barry R. Bloom, "A Perspective on AIDS Vaccines," *Science*, June 28, 1996, p. 1,888.

96. Christine Gorman, "The Exorcists," *Time*, Fall 1996, (special issue), p. 66.

97. Jon Cohen, "Looking for Leads in HIV's Battle with the Immune System," *Science*, May 23, 1997, p. 1,196.

98. Quoted in Andrew Lawler and Jon Cohen, "A Deadline for an AIDS Vaccine," *Science*, May 23, 1997, p. 1,184.

99. Quoted in Lawler and Cohen, "A Deadline for an AIDS Vaccine," p. 1,185.

100. McCoy and Inciardi, *Sex, Drugs, and the Continuing Spread of AIDS*, p. 161.

Glossary

AIDS (acquired immunodeficiency syndrome): The most severe stage of disease resulting from infection by the human immunodeficiency virus (HIV).

antibodies: Proteins in the blood that seek out and attach themselves to foreign substances in the blood, marking the invaders for destruction by other parts of the immune system.

AZT (also known as Retrovir or zidovudine): The first antiviral drug treatment used for managing HIV infection.

clinical trials: Tests of new drugs or vaccines on humans under controlled conditions; often one group gets an experimental drug and another group gets a placebo (or inactive substance).

CMV: A herpes infection due to a virus (*Cytomegalovirus*) that often causes death in people with AIDS.

combination therapy: The use of two or more drugs as treatment; the combination of drugs is commonly called a drug cocktail.

condom: A latex sheath that fits snugly over an erect penis to prevent pregnancy and transmission of disease-causing viruses and bacteria.

contagion: Transmission of a disease from one person to another through contact.

diagnosis: The determination by a doctor or clinic of the presence of a specific disease or infection.

epidemic: An outbreak of disease that affects many individuals within a population.

hemophilia: An inherited disease that prevents the normal clotting of blood.

HIV (human immunodeficiency virus): The virus that causes AIDS.

HIV disease: A variety of symptoms and signs found in people who are HIV-positive.

immune deficiency: A breakdown or inability of certain parts of the immune system to function, making a person vulnerable to disease.

immune system: The body's natural defender against disease.

Kaposi's sarcoma: A tumor commonly occurring in people with AIDS; usually shows up as painless spots on the skin, colored a characteristic pink or purple.

lymph nodes: Small bean-sized organs that act as filters for the immune system.

opportunistic infection: Certain illnesses, often life-threatening, that afflict people with AIDS; the organisms that cause these illnesses take advantage of the "opportunity" of a weakened immune system to cause damage.

pandemic: An outbreak of a disease occurring over a wide geographic area and affecting a relatively high proportion of the population.

placebo: A substance that has no effect on the body, given to one group of experimental subjects, while another group receives a drug being tested during clinical trials of proposed drug treatments.

***Pneumocystis carinii* pneumonia (PCP):** A severe form of pneumonia and the most common life-threatening infection in AIDS patients.

protease inhibitor: A drug that interferes with a crucial stage in the HIV life cycle.

resistance: The acquired ability of a microorganism to overcome a drug administered to combat it; usually occurs when a microorganism develops new strains that are unaffected by the drug.

retrovirus: A particularly powerful class of viruses that includes HIV.

reverse transcriptase: An enzyme that performs an essential step in the life cycle of HIV.

T-helper cells: Cells that trigger and stimulate an immune response in the body; HIV kills or disables these cells.

vaccine: A substance, usually injected, that protects an individual from a given disease.

virus: The smallest known infectious organism.

wasting syndrome: Progressive, involuntary weight loss associated with advanced HIV infection.

Organizations to Contact

The following organizations work in some area that concerns AIDS and AIDS-related issues. All offer publications and information to anyone interested in knowing more about HIV and AIDS.

Adolescent AIDS Program
Montefiore Medical Center
Albert Einstein College of Medicine
111 E. 210th St.
Bronx, NY 10467
(718) 882-0023

This organization offers information to teenagers about HIV and AIDS and about ways of preventing its spread. It publishes *Trading Fears for Facts: A Guide for Young People.*

American Civil Liberties Union (ACLU)
125 Broad St., 18th Fl.
New York, NY 10004
(212) 944-9800
Internet: http://www.aclu.org

The ACLU is the nation's oldest and largest civil liberties organization. Its Lesbian and Gay Rights/AIDS Project deals with legal issues, education, and public policy work on behalf of gays and lesbians. It publishes the handbook *The Rights of Lesbians and Gay Men.*

American Foundation for AIDS Research (AmFAR)
733 Third Ave., 12th Fl.
New York, NY 10097

(212) 682-7440
fax: (212) 682-9812
Internet: http://www.amfar.org

AmFAR supports AIDS prevention and research and speaks out on AIDS-related public policy. Its publications include the *AIDS/HIV Treatment Directory*, published twice a year, the newsletter *HIV/AIDS Educator and Reporter*, published three times a year, and the quarterly *AmFAR Newsletter*.

American Red Cross AIDS Education Office
1709 New York Ave. NW, Suite 208
Washington, DC 20006
(202) 434-4074
e-mail: info@usa.redcross.org
Internet: http://www.redcross.org

The Red Cross is one of America's oldest public health organizations. Its AIDS Education Office publishes pamphlets, brochures, and posters containing facts about AIDS. These and other materials are available at local Red Cross chapters. Local chapters also conduct presentations and operate speakers' bureaus.

Center for Women Policy Studies (CWPS)
1211 Connecticut Ave. NW, Suite 312
Washington, DC 20036
(202) 872-1770
fax: (202) 296-8962
e-mail: HN4066@handsnet.org

The CWPS was the first national policy institute to focus specifically on issues affecting the social, legal, and economic status of women. It believes that the government and the medical community have neglected the effect of AIDS on women and that more action should be taken to help women who have AIDS. The center publishes the book *The Guide to Resources on Women and AIDS* and produces the video *Fighting for Our Lives: Women Confronting AIDS*.

Centers for Disease Control and Prevention (CDC)
National AIDS Clearinghouse

PO Box 6003
Rockville, MD 20849-6003
(800) 458-5231
fax: (301) 738-6616
e-mail: aidsinfo@cdcnac.org
Internet: http://www.cdcnac.org

The CDC is the federal agency charged with protecting the nation's public health. It is the lead agency for prevention and control of diseases and public health emergencies. The CDC National AIDS Clearinghouse is a reference, referral, and distribution service for a wide range of information on HIV and AIDS. The CDC publishes information about AIDS in the *HIV/AIDS Prevention Newsletter,* and it includes updates on the disease in its *Morbidity and Mortality Weekly Report.*

Family Research Council
700 13th St. NW, Suite 500
Washington, DC 20005
(202) 393-2100
fax: (202) 393-2134
e-mail: corrdept@frc.org
Internet: http://www.frc.org

The Family Research Council promotes the traditional family unit and the Judeo-Christian value system. The council opposes condom distribution programs and discussion of homosexuality in the nation's schools. Its members believe these programs and discussions promote sexual promiscuity and lead to the spread of AIDS. It publishes numerous reports, including the monthly newsletter *Washington Watch,* the bimonthly journal *Family Policy,* and *Free to Be Family,* a 1992 report that addresses issues ranging from sex education and teen sex to sexually transmitted diseases.

Focus on the Family
8605 Explorer Dr.
Colorado Springs, CO 80995
(719) 531-3400 or (800) 232-6459
fax: (719) 548-4525
Internet: http://harvest.reapernet.com/fof/page18.html

Focus on the Family, which promotes Christian values and strong family ties, campaigns against laws that specifically guarantee civil rights for homosexuals. It publishes the monthly magazines *Focus on the Family* and *Focus on the Family Citizen* for parents, children, and educators. It also publishes the video *Sex, Lies, and . . . the Truth*, a film that encourages abstinence and blames safe sex messages for increasing the spread of AIDS.

Gay Men's Health Crisis
Publications/Education Dept.
119 W. 24th St.
New York, NY 10011-0022
(212) 337-1950
fax: (212) 367-1220
Internet: http://www.gmhc.org

The Gay Men's Health Crisis provides support services, education, and advocacy for men, women, and children with AIDS. The group produces the cable television news program *Living with AIDS* and publishes *Treatment Issues*, a monthly newsletter that discusses experimental AIDS treatments. It also publishes *Treatment Fact Sheets* and the newletters *Lesbian AIDS Project* and *Notes*.

Harvard AIDS Institute
651 Huntington Ave.
Boston, MA 02115
(617) 432-4400
fax: (617) 432-4545

The Harvard AIDS Institute promotes awareness of HIV prevention, transmission, diagnosis, and treatment and supports AIDS education on local, national, and international levels. It works to provide multidisciplinary AIDS training to scientists and clinicians worldwide and supports policies and solutions that benefit those affected by HIV and AIDS. The institute publishes the newsletter *Harvard AIDS Review* twice a year.

National AIDS Fund
1730 K St. NW, Suite 815
Washington, DC 20006
(202) 408-4848
Internet: http://www.aidsfund.org

The National AIDS Fund seeks to eliminate HIV as a major health and social problem. Its members work with both the public and private sectors to provide care and strengthen prevention efforts through advocacy, grants, research, and education. The fund publishes the monthly newletter *News from the National AIDS Fund*, which is also available through the organization's website.

National Association of People with AIDS (NAPWA)
1413 K. St. NW
Washington, DC 20005-3442
(202) 898-0414
fax: (202) 898-0435
e-mail: napwa@thecure.org
Internet: http://www.thecure.org

NAPWA represents people with HIV. The association believes that every person with HIV has a right to health care, adequate housing, protection from violence, freedom from discrimination, the ability to travel and immigrate without regard to HIV status, and a dignified death. The association publishes a variety of materials, including the annual *Community Report*.

National Institute of Allergy and Infectious Diseases (NIAID)
Office of Communications
Bldg. 31, Rm. 7A-50
31 Center Dr. MSC 2520
Bethesda, MD 20892-2520
(301) 496-5717
fax: (301) 402-0120
Internet: http://www.niaid.nih.org

NIAID, a component of the National Institutes of Health, supports research aimed at preventing, diagnosing, and treating diseases such as AIDS. NIAID publishes education materials including the booklet *Understanding the Immune System* and fact sheets describing developments in AIDS drugs and vaccines and the effects of AIDS on women, children, and minority populations.

People with AIDS Coalition (PWA)
50 W. 17th St., 8th Fl.
New York, NY 10011
(212) 647-1415 or (800) 828-3280
fax: (212) 647-1419

The People with AIDS Coalition provides a hot line for AIDS treatment information and peer counseling for individuals with AIDS. The coalition publishes *PWA Newsline*, a monthly magazine containing treatment information, news analysis, and features on people living with AIDS. It also publishes *SIDAhora*, a Spanish/English quarterly concerned with AIDS in the Hispanic community.

Rockford Institute
934 N. Main St.
Rockford, IL 61103
(815) 964-5053
e-mail: rkfdinst@bossnt.com

The institute seeks to rebuild moral values and strengthen the American family. It believes that AIDS is a symptom of the decline of the traditional family and that the only way to eliminate AIDS is to support traditional families and moral behavior. The institute publishes the periodicals *Family in America* and the *Religion & Society Report*.

Sex Information and Education Council of the United States (SIECUS)
130 W. 42nd St., Suite 350
New York, NY 10036
(212) 819-9770

fax: (212) 819-9776
e-mail: siecus@aol.com
Internet: http://www.siecus.org

SIECUS is an organization of educators, physicians, social workers, and others who support the individual's right to acquire knowledge of sexuality and encourage responsible sexual behavior. The council promotes comprehensive sex education that includes AIDS education, teaching about homosexuality, and instruction about contraceptives and sexually transmitted diseases. It publishes fact sheets, the booklet *Talk About Sex*, the bimonthly *SIECUS Report*, and the books *Winning the Battle: Developing Support for Sexuality and HIV/AIDS Education* and *How to Talk to Our Children About AIDS*.

Suggestions for Further Reading

Loren Acker, Bram C. Goldwater, and William H. Dyson, *AIDS-Proof Your Kids: A Step-by-Step Guide*. Hillsboro, OR: Beyond Words Publishers, 1992. A no-nonsense guide for parents and kids, with plain and direct answers about the way AIDS is transmitted.

Deborah Davis, *My Brother Has AIDS*. New York: Atheneum Books, 1994. An excellent work of fiction, showing in great detail the agony a family goes through when one of its members is diagnosed with AIDS.

Barbara H. Draimin, *Coping When a Parent Has AIDS*. New York: Rosen, 1994. A clear and thoughtful discussion of the changes and problems a young person will face as a result of a parent's illness. Dispels rumors and myths about HIV and AIDS.

Lorna Greenberg, *AIDS: How It Works in the Body*. New York: Franklin Watts, 1992. Explains the causes of the disease, how the immune system works, and what happens when HIV attacks the immune system.

Tom Flynn and Karen Lound, *AIDS: Examining the Crisis*. Minneapolis: Lerner, 1995. A concise and easy-to-read discussion of HIV and AIDS, with chapters on prevention, transmission, and where the future may lead.

Judith C. Galas, *Gay Rights*. San Diego: Lucent Books, 1996. One chapter in this readable book discusses the major legal, medical, and emotional challenges faced by gay men who have HIV and AIDS.

Margaret O. Hyde and Elizabeth H. Forsyth, *AIDS: What Does It Mean to You?* New York: Walker, 1996. An easy-to-understand look at the many facets of AIDS, including behavior that increases the risk of contracting HIV, feelings about AIDS, life with AIDS, and recent developments in treatment and prevention.

———, *Know About AIDS*. New York: Walker, 1994. A readable book with a frank discussion on the ways the AIDS virus can be transmitted. Good discussion of AIDS testing and procedures as well as how AIDS has been handled by schools and families.

Earvin "Magic" Johnson, *What You Can Do to Avoid AIDS*. New York: Times Books, 1992. An inspirational, straightforward book by the much-loved former player for the Los Angeles Lakers. The book includes a discussion about behaviors that increase the likelihood of contracting HIV and the importance of acting responsibly for one's own sake and the sake of others.

C. Everett Koop and Timothy Johnson, *Let's Talk: An Honest Conversation on Critical Issues*. Grand Rapids, MI: Zondervan, 1992. Notable mainly for a chapter on AIDS in which Koop, a former U.S. surgeon general, presents his thoughts on AIDS and the desperate need for widespread education and prevention efforts.

Leonard J. Martelli, Fran D. Peltz, William Messina, and Steven Petrow, *When Someone You Know Has AIDS: A Practical Guide*. New York: Crown Trade Paperbacks, 1993. Although not specifically written for teen readers, this book offers valuable ideas, information, and solace to anyone who knows someone with AIDS.

Tolbert McCarroll, *Morning Glory Babies: Children with AIDS and the Celebration of Life*. New York: St. Martin's Press, 1988. Although this book was published some time ago, it presents a unique and true look at three babies with AIDS and the small community that cared for them.

Alvin Silverstein and Virginia Silverstein, *AIDS: The Deadly Threat.* Hillside, NJ: Enslow, 1991. A broad look at HIV and AIDS, including prevention, treatment, facts about transmission, and how different people cope with the disease.

Gail B. Stewart, *People with AIDS*. San Diego: Lucent Books, 1996. A fascinating look at the lives of four people who have HIV or AIDS. The author's in-depth interviews with each of her subjects provide a uniquely personal and human look at life with AIDS.

Ryan White and Anne Marie Cunningham, *Ryan White: My Own Story*. New York: Dial Press, 1991. The moving story of the boy who contracted HIV through routine treatment for hemophilia and was then ostracized by the community in which he lived.

Works Consulted

Laura Beil, "AMA Backs HIV Test for Pregnant Women," *Dallas Morning News*, June 28, 1996.

Amanda Bennett, "A New Regimen: Africa's AIDS Experts Turn to Antibiotics to Slow the Epidemic," *Wall Street Journal*, December 27, 1996.

Michael D. Biskup and Karin L. Swisher, eds., *AIDS*. San Diego: Greenhaven Press, 1992.

Barry R. Bloom, "A Perspective on AIDS Vaccines," *Science*, June 28, 1996.

Elinor Burkett, *The Gravest Show on Earth: America in the Age of AIDS*. Boston: Houghton Mifflin, 1995.

Chandler Burr, "The AIDS Exception: Privacy vs. Public Health," *Atlantic Monthly*, June 1997.

Dana Calvo, "Advances in U.S. AIDS Treatments Bad News for Victims in Mexico," *Corpus Christi Caller Times* (from the Associated Press), March 22, 1997.

Marlene Cimmons, "AIDS Deaths Drop Further, U.S. Reports," *Los Angeles Times*, July 15, 1997.

Jon Cohen, "AIDS Mood Upbeat—for a Change," *Science*, February 17, 1995.

———, "At Conference, Hope for Success Is Further Attenuated," *Science*, November 18, 1994.

———, "Bumps on the Vaccine Road," *Science*, September 2, 1994.

———, "Looking for Leads in HIV's Battle with the Immune System," *Science*, May 23, 1997.

———, "Planned Tests in Thailand Spark Debate," *Science*, May 23, 1997.

———, "Results on New AIDS Drugs Bring Cautious Optimism," *Science*, February 9, 1996.

———, "Thailand Weighs AIDS Vaccine Tests," *Science*, November 10, 1995.

"Coming Clean About Needle Exchange," *Lancet*, November 25, 1995.

Charles P. Cozic, ed., *The AIDS Crisis*. San Diego: Greenhaven Press, 1991.

"Death by Denial," *Lancet*, June 17, 1995.

Paul Harding Douglas and Laura Pinsky, *The Essential AIDS Fact Book*. New York: Pocket Books, 1996.

Max Essex, "Confronting the AIDS Vaccine Challenge," *Technology Review*, October 1994.

Robin Estrin, "More AIDS Hospices Close Doors," *Corpus Christi Caller Times* (from the Associated Press), January 26, 1997.

Judy Foreman, "Decline in Deaths from AIDS Is Noted," *Corpus Christi Caller Times* (from the *Boston Globe*), February 28, 1997.

Helene D. Gayle, "Letters: The AIDS Exception," *Atlantic Monthly*, September 1997.

Josie Glausiusz, "AIDS: The Pandemic Continues," *Discover*, January 1997.

Christine Gorman, "The Disease Detective," *Time*, December 30, 1996/January 6, 1997.

———, "The Exorcists," *Time*, Fall 1996 (special issue).

Mirko D. Grmek, *History of AIDS: Emergence and Origin of a Modern Pandemic*. Princeton, NJ: Princeton University Press, 1990.

Daniel Q. Haney, "AIDS Vaccine May Work—if Researchers Ever Dare Test It on Humans," *Corpus Christi Caller Times* (from the Associated Press), May 25, 1997.

Nat Hentoff, "Censoring the Right to Live," *Progressive*, February 1995.

Tracey Hooker and Dianna Gordon, "Mothers and AIDS," *State Legislatures*, April 1995.

"International Disunity on HIV Vaccine Efficacy Trials," *JAMA*, October 12, 1994.

Brian Kearney and Steven Petrow, *The HIV Drug Book*. New York: Pocket Books, 1995.

Patricia Kloser and Jane MacLean Craig, *The Woman's HIV Sourcebook*. Dallas: Taylor Publishing, 1994.

Richard Lacayo, "Hope with an Asterisk," *Time*, December 30, 1996/January 6, 1997.

Andrew Lawler and Jon Cohen, "A Deadline for an AIDS Vaccine," *Science*, May 23, 1997.

Barbara J. Ledeen, "Sacrificing Babies on the Altar of Privacy," *Wall Street Journal*, August 3, 1995.

Daniel A. Leone, ed., *The Spread of AIDS*. San Diego: Greenhaven Press, 1997.

William H. Masters, Virginia E. Johnson, and Robert C. Kolodny, *Crisis: Heterosexual Behavior in the Age of AIDS*. New York: Grove Press, 1988.

Clyde B. McCoy and James A. Inciardi, *Sex, Drugs, and the Continuing Spread of AIDS*. Los Angeles: Roxbury Publishing, 1995.

Laurie McGinley, "Medicine: States Move to Ration Promising AIDS Drugs," *Wall Street Journal*, August 22, 1996.

Andrew Purvis, "The Global Epidemic," *Time*, December 30, 1996/January 6, 1997.

Paul Recer, "Panel Urges Use of Sex Education as Weapon Against AIDS Epidemic," *Corpus Christi Caller Times* (from the Associated Press), February 14, 1997.

"Released Report Says Needle Exchanges Work," *JAMA*, April 5, 1995.

Sarah Richardson, "AIDS: Crushing HIV," *Discover*, January 1997.

Tamara L. Roleff and Charles P. Cozic, eds., *AIDS*. San Diego: Greenhaven Press, 1998.

Mary Romeyn, *Nutrition and HIV: A New Model for Treatment*. San Francisco: Jossey-Bass Publishers, 1995.

David Sanford, "Back to a Future: One Man's AIDS Tale Shows How Quickly Epidemic Has Turned," *Wall Street Journal*, November 8, 1996.

Deborah L. Shelton, "No Place on Earth Untouched," *American Medical News*, December 16, 1996.

Philip Shenon, "AIDS Epidemic, Late to Arrive, Now Explodes in Populous Asia," *New York Times*, January 21, 1996.

H. R. Shepherd, "Still Needed: An AIDS Vaccine," *Wall Street Journal*, December 3, 1996.

Randy Shilts, *And the Band Played On: Politics, People, and the AIDS Epidemic*. New York: St. Martin's Press, 1987.

Julie Shippen, "AIDS Rates Rising for 30- to 40-Year-Old Heterosexual Women," *Corpus Christi Caller Times* (from Knight-Ridder news service), August 29, 1996.

Helen Mathews Smith, "The Deadly Politics of AIDS," *Wall Street Journal*, October 25, 1995.

Deborah Sontag, "HIV Testing for Newborns Debated Anew," *New York Times*, February 10, 1997.

James L. Sorensen, *Preventing AIDS in Drug Users and Their Sexual Partners*. New York: Guilford Press, 1991.

Jeff Stryker, Thomas J. Coates, and Pamela DeCarlo et al., "Prevention of HIV Infection: Looking Back, Looking Ahead," *JAMA*, April 12, 1995.

Harold Varmus, "There's No Imbalance in AIDS Research," Letter to the editor, *New York Times*, January 10, 1997.

Michael Waldholz, "Combined-Drug Therapy Being Hailed as Promising Weapon in AIDS Battle," *Wall Street Journal*, July 8, 1996.

———, "Drug Withdrawal: Dr. Ho's Next Step in AIDS Research Is a Remarkable Gamble," *Wall Street Journal*, December 17, 1996.

———, "Medicine: Some AIDS Cases Defy New Drug 'Cocktails,'" *Wall Street Journal*, October 10, 1996.

———, "Strong Medicine: New Drug 'Cocktails' Mark Exciting Turn in the War on AIDS," *Wall Street Journal*, June 14, 1996.

———, "Technology & Health: For First Time, Drug 'Cocktail' Seems to Eliminate HIV in Its Hiding Places," *Wall Street Journal*, November 7, 1996.

Rick Weiss, "Experimental AIDS Vaccine Prevents Virus in Monkeys," *Washington Post*, April 30, 1997.

Bruce G. Weniger and Max Essex, "Clearing the Way for an AIDS Vaccine," *New York Times*, January 4, 1997.

Index

Ackerman, Gary, 48
Acquired Immunodeficiency Syndrome. *See* AIDS
Africa, sub-Saharan, 54–55, 56, 60, 62–63, 75
AIDS
  causes of, 19–22
  controversy over, 6–8, 32
    see also HIV testing, debate over; needle exchange
  deaths caused by, 8, 65
  first cases of, 11–12
  first reactions to, 16–17
  prevention, 24–26
    see also education; risk reduction; vaccine
  spread of, in developing countries, 54–60
  efforts to control, 60–63
  treatment. *See* drug treatments
  see also HIV
American Academy of Pediatrics, 52
American College of Obstetricians and Gynecologists, 52
American Medical Association, 51–52

antibiotics, 62–63
AZT, 7–8, 45, 50, 66–68, 71
  problems with, 68–69

babies. *See* infants
blood
  banks, 37–38, 42
  HIV spread through contact with, 20–21, 23, 24
Burma, 55

cancer, 14–15, 67, 68
Center for Population Options, 31
Centers for Disease Control and Prevention (CDC), 13, 65
  policy on HIV testing, 42–43, 48, 51
  research on AIDS, 17–21
  study of needle exchange, 30
children
  AIDS education for, 30–35
  infected with AIDS, 56–57
  see also infants
Clinton, Bill, 80–81
Coburn, Tom, 45, 48
Colorado, 43
condoms, 26–27, 59

education on use of, 32, 33, 34–35

drug treatments, 62–64, 69–71
  cost of, 58, 74–75
  effect of, 65–66
  failure of, 73–74
  limitations of, 72–73
  success of, 71–72
  see also AZT
drug users, 18, 19, 23, 27–28
  see also needle exchange

education, AIDS
  as opposed to HIV testing, 44–45
  opposition to, 59
  public, 35–36
  for youth, 30–35
Europe, Western, 56

gay community, 11, 18, 21
  AIDS found in, 56
  fears discrimination, 40–42
  reactions to AIDS, 16–17
Global AIDS Strategy, 60–61

hemophilia, 20, 21–22
hepatitis B, 19
heterosexuals, 19–20, 21, 56
HIV, 6, 22–23
  is complex virus, 77–78
  treatment for, 45, 69–74
  U.S. infections per year, 24

  see also HIV testing
HIV Prevention Act of 1997, 45
HIV testing, 37
  could determine sexual orientation, 41–42
  debate over, 38–39, 44
  in developing countries, 58
  for infants, 47–48
  disclosure of results, 48–50
  opposition to mandatory, 44
  for pregnant women, 45–47, 51
  prenatal, 50–53
  voluntary and anonymous, 42–43
homosexuals. *See* gay community
human immunodeficiency virus. *See* HIV

immune system, 22–23
  destruction of, 12–14, 17, 19, 73
  rebuilding, 72
India, 54, 55–56, 74
Indonesia, 59
infants,
  HIV testing for, 47–51
  number of HIV-positive, 49, 55

Kaposi's sarcoma, 14–17, 19

Los Angeles, 12–14, 18, 19

Malaysia, 59
Mayersohn, Nettie, 47–48
Mayo Clinic, 20–21
Minnesota, 43

National Institutes of Health (NIH), 30, 77, 78, 80
needle exchange, 27, 28–30
needle sharing, 20, 23, 28
Newborn Infant HIV Notification Act, 47–48
New York, 43
  HIV testing in, 48–51
New York City, 14–15, 18

PCP. *See Pneumocystis carinii* pneumonia
Pneumocystis carinii pneumonia (PCP), 12, 16–17, 18, 19, 20
pregnant women, counseling for, 45–47
prostitution, 27
protease inhibitors, 45, 69–72
  failure of, 73–74

refugees, 60
research, AIDS, 21–23
  drug, 7–8
  funding for, 76–77
  for vaccine, 78–81
  see also Centers for Disease Control and Prevention
retroviruses, 22

risk reduction
  through education, 30–36
  through needle exchange, 27–30
  through sexual abstinence, 32–34
  see also safe sex

safe sex, 34–35
San Francisco, 18
sexual abstinence, 32–34
sexual contact,
  AIDS is spread through, 24
sexually transmitted disease, 11
  AIDS as, 19–20, 21
  testing for, 38, 39–40
sexual practices, 25–26
  heterosexual vs. homosexual, 56
  in youth, 31–32
syphilis, 40, 51

teen pregnancy, 33
Thailand, 54, 55–56, 62, 74
  test vaccines, 79
T-helper cells, 13

United Nations, 60
United States, 56, 57, 58, 63
unprotected sex, 26
U.S. Agency for International Development (USAID), 63
U.S. Department of Health and Human Services, 36

U.S. Food and Drug
  Administration, 67

vaccines, 62, 65, 76–77,
  78–81

Wellikoff, Rick, 15–16

White House Office on
  National AIDS Policy, 31
women
  infected with AIDS, 26, 55,
    56–57, 61
World Health Organization,
  57, 58, 60–61

Picture Credits

Cover photo: © Mark Phillips/Photo Researchers, Inc.
Mark Ahlstrom, 9, 80
AP Photo/CNA, Wang Fei-hua, 70
AP Photo/Jerome Delay, 76
AP Photo/Jack Kustron, 69
AP Photo/Mark Lennihan, 75
AP Photo/Gene J. Puskar, 21
© Donna Binder/Impact Visuals, 30
© Alan Clear/Impact Visuals, 31
© J. Kirk Condyles/Impact Visuals, 26
© F. Duran/Sipa Press, 67
© Tom Ferenztz/Impact Visuals, 14
© Harvey Finkle/Impact Visuals, 44
© J. P. G./Sipa Press, 79
© Giannroni/Sipa Press, 59
© Marilyn Humphries/Impact Visuals, 34
© Rick Gerharter/Impact Visuals, 7
© Andrew Lichtenstein/Impact Visuals, 18, 46, 52
© Mark Peters/Sipa Press, 61
© Ed Peters/Impact Visuals, 64
© Alon Reininger/Contact Press Images/Woodfin Camp & Associates, Inc., 42
© Wallis Robert/Sipa Press, 50
© Reuters/Corbis-Bettmann, 56
© Lonny Shavelson/Impact Visuals, 66
© Catherine Smith/Impact Visuals, 27
© Howard Sochurek/Woodfin Camp & Associates, Inc., 23
UPI/Corbis-Bettmann, 39
© A. Ramey/Woodfin Camp & Associates, Inc., 62

About the Author

Lori Shein is an editor and writer. She has been editing books for young readers for about seven years. Before becoming an editor, she spent ten years reporting and writing for newspapers. She lives in San Diego, California.